I Have Come
on a Lonely Path:
Memoir of a Shaman

By Kim Keum-Hwa
with Kim Hye-Kyoung

Alpha Sisters Publishing, LLC
5174 McGinnis Ferry Road #348
Alpharetta, GA 30005
alphasisterspublishing.com

This book is published with the support of the Literature Translation Institute of Korea (LTI Korea).

Written by Kim Keum-Hwa, Kim Hye-Kyoung
Translator: Peace Pyunghwa Lee, Seo Choi
Editor: E. Ce Miller
Publisher: Seo Choi
Book Designer: Sheenah Freitas
Publishing Consultation and Author Photography: Chanho Park

Library of Congress Cataloging-in-Publication Data is available upon request.

First Edition
ISBN 979-8-9869373-2-8 (Paperback)
ISBN 979-8-9869373-3-5 (e-book)

Printed in the United States of America

To Divine Spirit

Content Warning:
This book contains stories of domestic abuse, physical violence, war, mental illness, suicide, poverty, police brutality, and discrimination. Please read with care.

A Note About the Title:
The title of this memoir, *I Have Come on a Lonely Path*, is the
English translation of the chant shaman Kim Keum-Hwa sang as
a young girl, embodied by Spirit, as she performed her *geollip*—a
rite of passage requiring a shaman-to-be to travel her village,
collecting donations of money, grain, and metals to be used in
preparing her initiation ritual. In Kim's North Korean dialect,
외기러왔소 is a beautiful and poignant phrase, making this title
a fitting way to honor the author and her lifelong dedication to
walking the solitary, often lonely path of a *mudang*.

Contents

Part 1:
A Divine Flower Abloom in the Human World

Part 2:
"Why Did You Become a Shaman?"

Part 3:
Let Us Share Blessings and Release the Bitterness of Han

Part 4:
A Lonely Path, A Mudang's Path

Part 5:
Following the Mudang's Path

Publisher's Note

Kim Keum-Hwa (1931–2019) was probably the most famous Korean shaman of our time. Born in a small village in the Hwanghae province of North Korea, Kim became an initiated shaman at the age of seventeen. After migrating to South Korea during the Korean War, she continued her life's work as a *mudang*—a Korean shaman—through decades of social, cultural, and economic transitions in modern Korea. Through her dedicated work performing Korean Shamanic Rituals—*"gut"*—and teaching the wisdom of our ancestors, she received international recognition and the designation of Korea's Intangible Cultural Property in the 1980s and continued her work until her death in 2019.

Her memoir, '비단꽃 넘세,' in its original form, was published in October 2007, and the 2014 film *Manshin*, directed by Park Chan-kyung, was inspired by its stories. Unfortunately, this beautiful book is no longer available anywhere in Korea since the publisher went out of business in 2011. Only a few original copies remain at her shrine, Keumhwa-dang, a place cherished by her disciples and led by her spirit daughter and niece, Kim Hye-Kyoung.

In 2018, I received Kim's memoir as a gift, by chance, having no idea who Shaman Kim Keum-Hwa was or what her history contained.

Or maybe nothing is by chance. Maybe it was divine guidance.

In 2018, during my meditations and prayers, I received downloads urging me to research Korean Shamanism and consider my path as a shaman of Korean descent. Before this time, I had been studying the Shamanic traditions of different cultures, yet I had deliberately chosen not to explore Korean Shamanism. Growing up in Korea in the seventies and eighties, I held onto a misguided belief that the Shamanism of my own ancestors, performed and led by *mudangs*, was too wild, too scary.

At the same time, I was also receiving guidance that I should write and publish my first book, which also felt too intimidating and wild to imagine—me, an author? Who was I to think I could write a book and that people would actually read it? But to become an author *and then* a Korean shaman? It felt like such an absurd, wild idea.

Still, the Divine Spirit can be quite persistent in guiding us on our intended paths. As soon as I surrendered to their guidance and started my research, I was introduced to a woman named Cheryl Pallant. Cheryl had just published a memoir called *Ginseng Tango* about the time she lived in Korea a decade prior, and in it, she had written about meeting and dancing with a very famous Korean shaman. And now, she lived in my hometown of Richmond, Virginia. What a coincidence!

I reached out to Cheryl, and our friendship grew from our first meeting. Cheryl had years of experience and wisdom as a poet, author, lightworker, healer, teacher, and all-around badass woman. As someone who was only a few years into my spiritual path and only contemplating my first book, Cheryl was an elder I hadn't known I needed, all of sudden guiding and encouraging me with generosity and wisdom.

During one of the days I spent at her house chatting about writing, spirituality, and anything else you might imagine, she gifted me a copy of '비단꽃 넘세.' During her time in Korea, Cheryl had been invited to Keumhwa-dang to watch Shaman Kim Keum-Hwa perform a ritual. During the ritual, Shaman Kim invited Cheryl to dance, placing a brightly-colored Shamanic robe around her shoulders and giving her a knowing smile—recognition that she, too, was a lightworker. After that memorable encounter, Cheryl was gifted a copy of Kim's memoir. Since it was written in Korean and Cheryl was unable to read it, she had simply kept the book all these years, safely in her bookcase, unread. When she handed the book to me, she said, "I think I was keeping this book for you."

Despite the serendipity of this encounter, I didn't actually read '비단꽃 넘세' until 2020. I wasn't ready to dig into the book. I was too intimidated, too green on my own path to feel ready to engage with Kim's story. It wasn't until 2020, after starting my micro-publishing company and publishing my first book and a set of oracle cards, that I finally read Kim Keum-Hwa's memoir.

Her memoir is such a beautiful collection of stories of one *mudang's* life, containing so much hard-won wisdom. Kim's memoir reads as though the esteemed elder shaman herself is sitting before the reader, generously sharing her stories and lessons. For me—and, I believe, for anyone embarking on their own spiritual path—*I Have Come on a Lonely Path: Memoir of a Shaman* is more than a memoir, but an invitation to sit at the feet of a wise one and absorb their teachings. Without a flesh-and-blood elder to guide me, Kim's memoir stepped into that void of wisdom I needed to fill.

In 2020, I shared a post on Instagram that I was finally reading Kim Keum-Hwa's book. Quickly, people from Korea started asking me where I had gotten the memoir since it was so rare and difficult to find. That's when I learned Kim's book had been out of print for over a decade!

How I got the chance to publish the book is another story of divine guidance. I was involved in another book project titled *Shrine*, which included photographing and documenting Korea's remaining Shamanic shrines and the shamans who are the keepers of those shrines and their traditions. Photographer Chanho Park captured the book's images, and scholar Sungje Cho provided the commentary and index at the end of the book. In *Shrine*, Kim Keum-Hwa and her successor, Kim Hye-Kyoung, had both been photographed.

When Chanho connected me to Shaman Kim Hye-Kyoung about the opportunity to publish her spirit mother's memoir, the fact that I had already established myself as a publisher, particularly one who'd translated and published two books on Korean's ancient wisdom and traditions, gave Kim Hye-Kyoung trust. In October 2022, fifteen years after the original memoir was first published and three years after Kim Keum-Hwa's passing, I was invited to Keumhwa-dang. In true Korean tradition, Shaman Kim and her spirit sisters first fed me and my fellow travelers a home-cooked Korean meal served at a low table. After lunch, we signed the publishing contract.

Afterward, Shaman Kim allowed us to wander the shrine and visit halls dedicated to specific gods, such as Sanshin and Chilseong-shin. To me, she said, "You probably want to see upstairs."

When I walked into the second floor of Keumhwa-dang, I found myself surrounded by Kim Keum-Hwa's portraits and performance photos, and a collection of all the shrine's Shamanic paintings, as well as an altar displaying all of the ritual tools Kim used throughout her life. I wish I could adequately describe my feelings then in words, but they exceed language. I felt her—Kim Keum-Hwa's presence. Alongside her presence, just as vividly, was the presence of her gods. They were not separate but together; the Shamanic deities she had served for seventy years and her own spirit felt like one—a single, powerful collective woosh of benevolent but fierce energy. The force of that powerful energy rushed through me as soon as I stood at the altar.

"선생님, 저 왔어요. 감사합니다."

"Teacher, Elder, I've come here. Thank you."

I bowed my head in awe and gratitude to the collective energy, the Divine Spirit, which had guided me on this path so far.

Looking back on the 'round-the-world journey this memoir took in order to get to me—the hands it passed through and the stories it told along the way—I feel there's no doubt this book was brought to me by Divine Spirit, gifted to me by a personal elder messenger at the beginning of my path as a Korean American shaman and a writer. Only after I followed the divine guidance to publish my own books and those of others, all about Korean ancestral wisdom and traditions, did I receive the opportunity to publish this memoir.

I'm especially moved that the Korean edition of Kim Keum-Hwa's memoir has been out of print for a decade—in light of the rarity of this text today, sharing her story and wisdom as medicine for the world, now available in English feels like nothing less than a divine mission: an offering to her and our ancestors.

This first English edition of *I Have Come on a Lonely Path: Memoir of a Shaman* includes new chapters written by Kim Hye-Kyoung, who has succeeded her aunt and spirit mother, Kim

Keum-Hwa, and continues to watch over Keumhwa-dang today. I pray that readers will find the memories and stories she has shared in the pages healing and inspiring.

    With this book, may you receive the innate wisdom of Divine Spirit as well...

Seo Choi
August 2023

Translator's Reflection

Psalm 84:5−7

Blessed are those whose strength is in God,
whose lives become roads God travels,
When they wind through the Valley of Weeping,
they make it a place of refreshing springs;
the early rain also covers it with blessings.
They go from strength to strength;
until the God of Gods will be seen atop the mountain!

I Have Come on a Lonely Path is a spiritual autobiography written by the late Kim Keum-Hwa, Korea's most nationally renowned *manshin*. After living for decades as an outcast, she was much belatedly recognized as a carrier of intangible cultural treasures. This memoir, published in her 60th year as an initiated and celebrated shaman, chronicles her harrowing life story against the backdrop of a cataclysmic Korean history—a country at once ravaged by Japanese occupation, war, ensuing division, and military occupation as well as western modernization. It is written in the intimate voice of a woman who has known deep pain and conveys the wisdom distilled from the decades she has served as a mediator between humans and gods.

It is a miracle that I got to participate in creating this book as an offering for the Korean diaspora. Reading Kim's memoir for the first time during the height of the COVID-19 pandemic as an Asian American feminist was profoundly healing. I longed for this book to be made available to the diaspora, and I am amazed that this dream is coming true. Spirit Grandmother Kim Keum-Hwa is North Korean, and her writing is filled with the sounds and accents of her northern home. I am grateful for the support I have received in translating unfamiliar words from Kim Hye-Kyoung and Lee Mi-Young, initiated *mudang*s carrying on our ancient sacred traditions.

This book was translated during a time of great transition for me personally, as my partner and I moved to another state to provide care for dying family members—a fairly common occurrence in the lives of many Asians, especially immigrants. It was a very bleak and cold season wherein, facing the death of loved ones, we had to make sense of the past and how historical traumas continue to animate the present. This book served as a living guide through the bitter mountain range I found myself climbing and helped me stay present to the mountain of death, to the mountain of accounting for and honoring a life, and to the mountain of staying committed to life even when it feels like the sky has fallen.

In painting the shaman's path as a lonely pilgrimage, Spirit Grandmother Kim Keum-Hwa reminds us that the human journey we each must take through life and death is paved with difficulty. Those who are weary and worn out from their respective journeys thus far would do well to remember that wanting to give up and finding themselves crumpled, defeated, and fallen is part of it. We are invited to "keep falling countless times and keep rising countless times." But for what do we keep enduring and keep rising?

I am haunted by the portrait of a beloved community that once was and can be again for our living. Kim portrays her hometown village of pre-war Northern Korea as a haven, a thriving community of *jeong* that ensured absolutely everyone in the village, down to the lonely old man and even the village ghosts, was remembered, accounted for, and fed during village feasts and holy days. Kim's deepest laments throughout the book are how people have forsaken sacred and human laws and turned away from each other. She was most passionate about upholding the traditions and ways of her ancestors, keeping their memories and sacred rituals alive.

Spirit Grandmother Kim Keum-Hwa serves as a living oracle to the pathway of divinity, inviting us to have faith that our ancestors and deities are here to remind us of our dignity and path forward. She invites us to a living communion with them and to trust that death is not the end. We continue because we are carried on and led ahead by the songs of our ancestors, and we know there is a heavenly feast waiting for those willing to travel far and wide to reach a place where one is known, remembered, and longed for.

There is a *gut*, a feast where humans are invited to stand in the presence of ancestors both human and divine, where truths are revealed and unveiled, grievances and pains aired and held, where reconciliations and forgiveness flower, and everyone is invited to a beautiful table of delicious food and rice cakes. There, those gathered are asked to dance under the whirling and colorful banners of Spirit, bespeaking joy and new life.

Peace Pyunghwa Lee
August 2023

Manshin's Path, Mediator of Gods and Humans

"Becoming a manshin *is to endure a lot of unbearable pain that no ordinary person can withstand."*

On the day I received *Naerim-gut*, my maternal grandmother, my spirit mother, held my hand and spoke those words, tears flowing endlessly from her eyes. I was just seventeen-years-old then, far too young to understand the path that lay ahead of me or the "unbearable pain" I was to endure. Simply knowing that god's words flooded my heart—words that others could not hear—filled me with overwhelming happiness.

But as years passed, I began to unravel the nature of the pain that my maternal grandmother spoke of. One by one, I discovered the pain of having to shoulder the worries of others, the pain of being the solver of all manner of problems in human lives, and the pain of being responsible for mediating and reconciling the relationships between humans and gods. There were desperate times when I had to risk my own life, and the sorrow of being ostracized because I was a *mudang* was indescribably deep.

There were many times when I resented the strenuous efforts of my life. I felt bitter towards Divine Spirit for placing such heavy burdens on me, and I resented the shallow heartlessness of those who only sought me out when they needed me. Countless tears were shed alone, turned away from others. Yet I endured all this suffering and bitterness because of my sense of responsibility and the fulfillment I found in my calling.

When a person deathly ill from a perplexing medical condition miraculously revived after coming to me, the sight of their once lifeless eyes gleaming with renewed vitality brought me a joy that could not be matched by anything in this world. The gratification of witnessing those who came to me to find relief from their worries and rejoice over discovering a solution to their troubles was indescribable. In hearing those I helped express their gratitude over and over again, I quietly repeated in my heart:

"Great Spirit, thank you so much."

It is the destiny of one chosen as a disciple of Divine Spirit to endure unbearable pain—but there too is a satisfaction that can only be obtained by doing so.

* * *

This year[1] is special to me in many ways. It marks the sixtieth year since I embarked on the path of a *mudang*, and it is also the year in

---

1. Kim Keum-Hwa wrote this prologue and the memoir in the fall of 2007, when '비단꽃넘세' was published.

which I will perform the *Mansudaetak-gut*[2] ritual after a decade-long hiatus.

My years living as a disciple of Spirit and as a woman are recorded here. Although I have many stories I wish to share, I am limited by the number of pages in this book. Still, it is my heart's steadfast desire to honestly recount the days of my past from beginning to end. When it came to stories I felt hesitant to share, I bolstered my courage by considering the encouragement I've received from others, notably my late teacher Zo Zayong and the late photographer Kim Soo-Nam. Each of these trailblazers served as a guide in promoting both myself and Korea's Shamanic culture to the world. I bow my head and offer deep gratitude to them. And although I cannot list them all, I wish to express my appreciation to everyone who worked hard to preserve the intangible cultural heritage of the *Hwanghae-do Daedong-gut*[3] and the *Seohae-an Poong-eo-je*[4] festivals, as well as Do-ol Yong-ok Kim and those who have strengthened and nurtured me personally.

In October, we plan to host a rich and vibrant *Mansudaetak-gut* at my shrine, Keumhwa-dang, on Ganghwa Island, which was built with the help of those who seek to preserve and cherish our Shamanic culture. Given our current difficulties both as a nation and as individuals,[5] my hopes and determination ahead of the ritual are also special.

Above all, my prayer for this ritual is that antagonism and

---

2. 만수대탁굿, a ritual performed for longevity and well-being of an elder, and, while the elder is still alive, for their ascent to the heavenly path after death.

3. 대동굿, a ritual performed for the well-being and prosperity for a larger village and community.

4. 서해안 풍어제, West Sea Abundant Fishing & Village Ritual, one of the traditional rituals protected as Intangible Cultural Property.

5. Great Recession of 2007–2009 also greatly impacted South Korean people.

conflicts will disappear and our country will become peaceful. I will offer my best efforts in praying that the difficulties gripping our nation will be smoothed out so that all the good-hearted people of Korea can flourish. I also earnestly pray for prosperity and blessings for the many people who cherish me and support Keumhwa-dang. To all those who are weary and weighed down by this brutal world, I sincerely hope they will receive the blessing that I, the shaman Kim Keum-Hwa, am offering and share that blessing with others.

* * *

When I look around me, I see many people leading worthy lives. It humbles me to see those who dedicate their lives to caring for kinless seniors, orphans, and children with disabilities. Their selfless acts of sacrifice for others make me wonder, *what have I done?*

Yet the overflowing interest and affection of those who respect and cherish Shamanic culture, care for me, hold my hand, bless my health, and encourage me to give me the courage to continue striving. Although I am passing my seventies and soon will be eighty-years-old, age is just a number marking my years in the realm of humans. In the days to come, as in the past, I will steadfastly walk the path of a *mudang*—a mediator between humans and gods.

Kim Keum-Hwa
Fall 2007

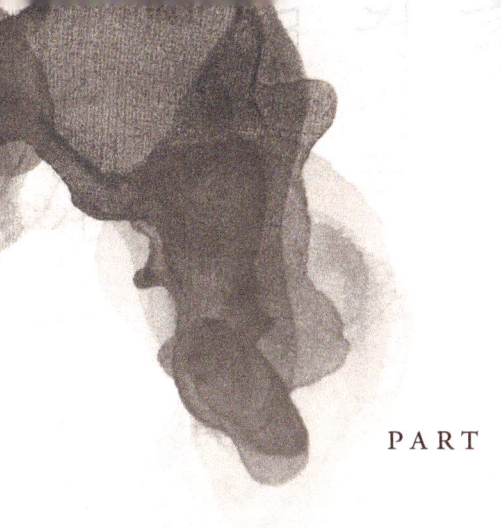

PART I

A Divine Flower Abloom in the Human World

For what reason did you become a shaman?

With a heart calcified in mute suffering, you
couldn't answer if you wanted to.

by Kim Keum-Hwa

ONE

A Worthless Second Daughter

My name, Keum-Hwa, means "silk flower." I was overjoyed when I received this name at the age of thirteen. Before that, my name was Neomse, which means "a younger brother is looking over her shoulder." My parents, who desperately yearned for a son, gave me this name when I was born a daughter. It was only natural that I hated that name when I was young.

My father was seventeen years older than my mother. She had been brought into the Kim family as the second daughter-in-law; more than anything else, her job was to produce sons who would continue the family lineage. However, her first child was a daughter, and the second also.

As soon as I let out my first cry, my aunt rushed to check if I was a boy or a girl.

"Another girl. One cunt after another!"

Upon hearing those words, my father turned away and sighed heavily as if the ground were about to give way.

"Just shove that useless girl out of sight." Without looking back, my father slammed the door and left.

Although my mother was disappointed to have birthed two daughters in a row, she was more disappointed by her husband's reaction. She carelessly wrapped me, a newborn babe, in a swaddling cloth and pushed me aside. However, a mother's love cannot be helped, and soon her heart softened.

How could I fault a baby? she thought. *Isn't this like murder?*

When my mother gingerly unwrapped the swaddling bundle she had carelessly shoved aside, she found that my entire body had turned blue, and I seemed out of breath. How much time had passed? But my complexion returned, and I narrowly survived death.

Still, the sorrow of a mother who had given birth to a series of unwelcome daughters was boundless. It was long after my delivery that my great-aunt finally brought food to my mother. Although a savory aroma of seaweed soup wafted from the pot, my mother's rice bowl was filled with a tangled mass of steamed young gourd vines instead of rice kernels. Deprived of postnatal care and recovery, she soon had to collect water from the well outside, travel to the stream to do laundry, and prepare her own meals. However, despite the afflictions she suffered, my mother felt sorrier for me, her daughter, who did not receive warm love and care.

Perhaps because my parents longed for a son so intensely, one night, they discovered they'd dreamed of a birth at the same time. Their vision was out of the ordinary.

In my mother's dream, heavy rain poured from the sky like a flood, thunder crashing and lightning striking all around. She went out into the yard and a pair of warrior general's swords fell from the sky right into her skirt. Meanwhile, my father dreamed he was sitting outside looking up at the sky while thunderbolts struck. There, he saw a blue dragon and a golden dragon entwined, piercing through the clouds and ascending into the sky amidst the storm. My parents thought for sure that this auspicious dream signaled a son. The elders in the household also eagerly waited for the moon to wax and for a son to be born.

But their expectations were high, and there was no avoiding the crushing disappointment that followed. Is that why, whenever my great uncle came to the house, he only coughed loudly and left without a word? Why the atmosphere of our home was such that my mother couldn't even nurse her baby comfortably? Why my mother lived as if she were sitting on a cushion of thorns?

One day, my maternal grandmother noticed my mother and me in our pitiable situation and said, "If you can give birth to a daughter, you will give birth to a son as well. At least, give her the name 'Neomse.'[6] Her brother is right behind her. Right?"

After that, my family called me "Neomse." Yet I always came last in our family.

The name Neomse finally paid off three years later when my mother gave birth to my younger brother. Once this son was born, the whole family rejoiced. Naturally, the disdain and neglect towards me lessened. I remember my great uncle carrying me on his back and holding my hand, happy to see my younger brother.

But, due to my family's poverty, that celebratory love was short-lived. My mother worked in the fields all day and did any other work she could to make a living. My older sister contributed to the housework by keeping the furnace lit and fetching water from the well with water jugs.

Eventually, another younger brother and a sister were born,

---

6. The name Neomse means "there is a younger brother peering over one's shoulder."

and I became burdened with the grueling task of carrying them around on my back all day. I was a child myself, small and weak, and whenever I carried the babies on my back, he or she would slip and hang on my hips. My siblings hung on my back all day long, even as my clothes became drenched with babies' urine. My only respite was when my mother nursed. In the summer, my back, waist, and buttocks festered from being drenched in sweat and urine. When my exposed raw flesh turned red and oozed blood, it stung and hurt greatly to carry the babies.

Callow and childish neighborhood children made a game of making fun of me. When I carried my siblings as I walked, children came in droves and circled around me.

"Look at you waddle here and wobble there, ready to tilt! *Neomse!*"

My stained and worn-out *jeogori* [7] and socks were so old that my toes stuck out, and my straw sandals were so tattered they were tied together with rope, so my appearance was pitiful. I should have felt sorrow as the neighborhood children mocked me while I struggled to carry my slumping siblings on my buttocks, but instead, I felt envy as I watched their raucous, playful gatherings.

Given my strife, how could I not be happy when "Neomse" finally became "Keum-Hwa"? At home, I was a useless, mistreated second daughter; outside, I was a lonely and pathetic "Neomse." Yet I was finally given the precious, pretty name "Keum-Hwa."

---

7. 저고리, a top of the traditional Korean *hanbok*.

TWO

Ommai, Let's Eat

My hometown is called Anbakkuni in the Seoksan township of the Yeonbaek district in Hwanghae Province. My father's surname is Kim, and his name comprises the characters "Taek" and "Geun." Our house in Anbakkuni was as small as a palm, with just one room and a tiny kitchen attached. When you opened the stubby straw door, you would find a small stone instead of a wooden floor. However, that house carried an unusual energy. At night, all sorts of strange sounds could be heard from the yard: the yard being swept with a straw broom, rice being winnowed and scooped into a bowl, and pebbles being loosened from a cart. The sounds were so clear and distinct—as if made by a person—that they were audible not just to my ears: everyone in the family heard those sounds.

At night, my father would light a cigarette from the brazier, puff on it, and say, "My goodness, the strange noises one hears. They sound just like humans."

In addition to our tiny home, our household was painfully destitute. One of my most vivid memories from my childhood years was clutching my always-famished stomach.

When I was very young, my parents took me with them to weed and forage in the mountain valleys. On days when just my parents would go to pluck weeds, I would follow them over a rocky hill.

My parents would crouch as if clinging to a steep hillside, picking the purplish millet drying in the sun; they could barely be grasped with two fingers. The valley where they foraged was gravel, and the hoe made clanging sounds when it hit the stones.

Foraging stubborn weeds from around the rocks, my parents would say, "Neomse-*ya*, if you feel sleepy, just lie down and sleep. We will call you to get up when it's time to eat. Be a good girl. That way, next year, we won't starve and will at least have some millet to eat."

Sitting in the field, looking at my parents, my mind was filled with thoughts like, *Will we ever be able to eat as much as we want?* My stomach constantly growled.

"Father, how much longer until we can eat?" I asked.

"Just a little while longer."

I waited a long time lying in the field, but I still did not hear the call to eat. As a young child, I could not gauge how long "a little while" really was. I was hungry, so I was consumed with thoughts of food.

"*Ommai*,[8] let's eat! Quickly! Huh?" I urged my mother.

My mother glanced at me and said, pointing in the distance, "We will eat when the shadow of that mountain reaches where you're sitting."

Then I would slump down in the field and wait for the distant mountain shadow to draw near, often falling asleep from

---

8. 오마이, North Korean dialect for mother.

exhaustion. After sleeping for some time, I heard my father's welcome voice.

"Neomse-*ya*, the area you are lying on is shaded. Come, get up. Let's eat."

Our meal consisted of just a whiff of plain yellow millet with *doenjang* (soybean paste) and *ganjang* (soy sauce). I didn't dare dream of meat. I wished to eat as many beans as I wanted, but even bean paste was severely rationed. Anytime we planted beans, they were planted on someone else's field—as sharecroppers, what we could bring home for ourselves was meager.

When I was young, my mother used to take me to collect brushwood, which we gathered because it burned well and there was little smoke, making it excellent firewood. By tying a wire perpendicular to a long stick, we pulled dead branches off of pine trees; the brittle branches resembled withered fingers and fell off with dull thuds. But gathering brushwood was not something we could do comfortably. Even if we were just picking up fallen brush from the ground, if seen by a Japanese police officer or forest service personnel, we would be arrested, the officers repeatedly shouting, "*Kono hito pagayaro!*"[9] That's why on the days we gathered the twigs in our skirts, we often returned home late in the evening, after the sun had set.

When I was seven-years-old, I was sent to my mother's family home. Although their situation was slightly better than that of my parents, when spring came, I still took to the fields and mudflats, looking for things to eat. I brought back wild greens, herbs, roots, and sometimes even oysters. In early spring, we foraged through fields. When we turned over the wild roots and dug deep enough, a thin sprout would emerge. These wild shoots tasted sweet when steamed over rice. I used to mix them with rice and serve them to my grandmother or make her a dish of freshly pulled sprouts.

---

9. "You stupid idiot!"

The streams also offered up things to eat. One could catch a crayfish lying flat on its stomach by digging around the areas where the ice had melted in a narrow and deep mountain valley or in a gently flowing sun-dappled creek. Lifting rocks from deep water, one might find a crayfish swimming with its tail stretched out. The large ones with lots of round eggs were steamed in a small pot with soy sauce until they turned bright red and had an appealing taste and appearance. However, crayfish was a dish reserved only for my grandmother or other adults, not given to us children.

Then, my father passed away when I was thirteen, and I was brought back home to do his share of farm work. When I went out to work in the furrows of the millet field with my mother in the scorching heat of summer's dog days, my entire body was drenched in sweat, my clothes suffocated my body, and my summer *jeogori* clung to my back with sweat. I sometimes collapsed, stretched out listlessly from hoeing. The fieldwork was grueling, and my persistent hunger made it even more depleting. Even after working all day under the blistering sun, the only meals I could find to fill my stomach were insubstantial millet or slippery barley rice served with soybean paste, red pepper paste, or soy sauce. Suffering from famishment, I couldn't get the thought of food out of my mind whether sleeping or awake.

Once, I overheard the adults speaking. At that time, the 12th Battalion of the Japanese Army rode around on large horses, hiring local laborers to load gravel into carts to lay new roads. They said if you followed them, they would give you a lunchbox made of rice mixed with red beans and throw foodstuff into the street for the laborers to collect. My ears perked up at the mention of the lunchbox, and I went out to search for where the Japanese soldiers hired local workers. While on my way, I met an elderly woman from my village who was also heading there, and we traveled together. After walking for a long while, we saw fully armed Japanese soldiers riding horses back and forth. They shouted in Japanese that we could not understand and even brandished whips. From their faces, they looked furious.

The old lady whispered, shocked, "Neomse, let's go home quickly. If we make a mistake here, we might get trampled to death by these Jap bastards."

She hurriedly grabbed my hand and dragged me along. She seemed extremely frightened; even her voice trembled.

"Don't even look their way. Let's go! Even ghosts may be killed here."

The old woman clutched my wrists so hard that they tingled with numbness. Despite being dragged away from that place, I could not shake my lingering attachment to the lunchbox. Tears threatened to spill as I thought of the rice with red beans. Throughout our journey, I had blissfully salivated at the thought of the rice, but now, returning empty-handed left me feeling pitiable and hollow. I even felt resentful and bitter toward the old woman who had pulled me away.

If I had gone alone, wouldn't I have been able to get at least one lunchbox? I thought. Perhaps someone might have thrown one my way, saying, "Child, who are you? Would you like to try this rice?"

It was a useless fantasy, but I felt utterly heartbroken, as if the lunchbox had evaporated right before my eyes. In those days, food was always scarce, and everyone went hungry. From the moment I opened my eyes in the morning, I was flooded with worries about the day's meal. All day, I toiled until my back was bent over in the fields just to survive. Now, so many years later, there is an overabundance of food in my life, but sometimes tears still come to my eyes when I hear the word "rice."

THREE

"This Strange *Eminai*,[9] Don't Play with Her!"

Despite growing up malnourished, I strangely grew taller than my peers. Every early spring and autumn, when I went to catch fish with other children at the beach, my hands were the quickest and my aim the most precise. We could find gobies in the holes next to the trough where the water churned. Sometimes, the gobies would stick their heads out of the hole as if waiting for us and then suddenly hide. When we put our hands into a hole, we could catch gobies the size of a child's forearm. Sometimes, when we reached deep for a goby without knowing what else lay in its hiding spot, oyster shells cut into our hands, drawing drops of red blood. I was also good at catching octopuses.

When we went to the beach together, people tried to quietly exclude me from catching something because I would spot and catch my target faster than anyone else. I was good at any game my peers played. Whether we were playing catch, throwing rag

10. 에미나이: North Korean dialect for woman or girl.

balls, jumping hopscotch, stick-tossing, or standing seesaw, I could jump higher and farther than anyone else. Whenever we made bets on our games, all the kids wanted to be on my side.

But at some point, I discovered I was becoming increasingly strange. While playing jacks, I would suddenly stop my hand in mid-air, with the feeling that someone was holding my hand. I threw stones and stared blankly at the tail stones without even thinking about catching them. When I played games, I would suddenly stop in my tracks at the sound of someone calling me or the energy of something blocking my way. On days when I would go as far as to idly mutter to myself, the other children were appalled. Sometimes, my body felt lethargic, like I was sinking to the ground, while other times, it felt weightless, as if I were floating—like my body wasn't mine and someone else was moving me. I didn't know why I was always sluggish yet couldn't sleep, anxious and nervous like a person who was constantly being chased. Without being conscious of it, I began talking to trees, stones, and water.

One evening, I walked up the nearby hill behind my house. The pine and oak trees that always stood there seemed to welcome me. I approached the tree and began speaking.

"Pine tree, how are you getting through this cold winter?" I said. "Spring is coming soon. Stand tall and smile. Don't be sorry for losing your leaves. Now you can talk to other trees and not be lonely."

As the wind blew and shook the pine tree, I stood before it and greeted it again.

"Oh, you're pleased to meet me? Why thank you, thank you."

When climbing up the mountain, I sometimes stopped my steps upon seeing a large, towering rock and asked, "Who are you waiting for, standing here endlessly like this?"

The rock couldn't respond, but I would brush my hand against its silent surface and talk to myself.

"Why are you silent? A secret? Okay. Then wait for me to come. Okay?"

Then, I would run, talking to myself.

"I am leaving. Without waiting. If you don't come, then so be it."

I wandered around strangely as if someone was summoning me, so there were many times when I ended up on unfamiliar paths without even realizing it. One day, after walking for a long time, I found myself standing in front of the township government office—located quite a distance from my neighborhood—without knowing why or how I ended up there. I turned my head to the sound of someone calling me and discovered a man from my neighborhood was looking at me.

"How did you end up all the way here?"

Startled, I told a lie. "I'm here to get the cowpox vaccine."

"Why would you get the cowpox vaccine again after already receiving the shot last year?" he asked.

"She said she's here to get vaccinated," an administrator beside my puzzled neighbor beckoned me. Thanks to my lie, I had to get another cowpox vaccine that day. I still have cowpox marks on both of my arms.

The adults in the neighborhood disliked me, saying I was a know-it-all. From the age of around ten or eleven, I had the urge to talk to people whenever I saw them. When something went missing in the neighborhood, I confidently claimed, "It's in so-and-so's yard." Or I would exclaim, "So-and-so is having an affair with so-and-so," without hesitation.

Once, to a friend I was playing with, I blurted out, "Hey, it looks like your father is going to pass away early." The adults disapproved of me for not being like an average child.

"What is wrong with that *eminai*? Don't play with her!"

Whenever I felt something, I would just say it without a second thought. People often clicked their tongues, saying I hardly behaved like a child should.

"Why do people hate me? I'm not what they think. I just want to help and be friendly, so why don't they understand my heart?"

It seemed like no one in the world—not my mother, father, neighbors, or friends—knew my heart, so I found it more comfortable to be alone. The more I was hurt by people, the more time I spent by myself. Though I still carried my younger siblings on my back and roamed through the hills and mountains, instead of people, I talked with trees and stones, the wind and flowers, opening my heart and becoming friends with them. I stopped paying attention to the reproaches and gossip of other people. After all, the world is made up of more than just people. It comforted me that the grass, flowers, trees, and water had all become my good friends.

The 14-Year-Old
New Bride Weeps Sadly

When I was fourteen-years-old, my maternal grandfather, whose house we had been living at, passed away. I tore my skirt to make *mombbae*[11] and wore them to the Women's Volunteer Corps[12] training. At home, it was whispered that I would be sent off to get married—people believed getting married was a way to avoid being drafted into the volunteer corps. One day, someone visited our home with the purpose of matchmaking, but I did not know what was what.

Our home could not afford a wedding feast. The groom's family

---

11. 몸빼바지, baggy drawstring pants.

12. The Korean Women's Volunteer Labor Corps was created to mobilize girls' and women's labor toward the Empire of Japan during the Japanese colonization of Korea. That said, the term "volunteer corps" was used interchangeably to signify comfort women or girls who were forced into sexual slavery by the Imperial Japanese Army.

sent five *mal*[13] of rice, a barrel of fabric, and two rolls of cotton cloth as wedding presents. I made a blanket and pillowcases from the fabric and undergarments and simple pants from the cotton cloth.

My wedding was held on the eighth day of the twelfth month of the Lunar Year, with snowflakes flickering as they fell from the sky. The groom, who was seventeen-years-old, arrived on a horse. In preparation for the feast, I had to fast for three days because defecating on one's wedding day was considered inappropriate. A ceremony was held in the yard, and I was placed in a palanquin. Inside the palanquin were a pair of straw sandals, a chamber pot, and a basket. I cried, calling for my deceased father, as I was carried away.

My husband's home was in a town called Small Boulder, about five *li*[14] away, and I cried throughout the whole journey. When the two young men carrying the palanquin laid it down, the young man in the front put his hands down before the young man in the back; they were not in sync, so the vehicle fell forward. I feared falling flat and met the ground with both hands instead. Tradition said it was not good for a new bride to touch the ground. All at once, an ominous feeling passed through me.

I arrived at my husband's home to find a drawn shade and an open folding screen in the yard. In front of a table set with an enormous feast, they performed something called *jagan-janchi*. Eighteen women, including myself, had to sit in a row to receive a table set with noodles, chicken legs, and pancakes while listening to blessings performed by an elderly man.

---

13. 말, a unit of volume equivalent to 18 liters.

14. 리, a unit of distance, roughly 500 meters.

The blessing of a daughter-in-law enters the Oh family's house,
Pumpkin-like prosperity piles in from the front mountain,
Mortar-like luck rolls in from the back mountain.

After entering the home, I sat numbly for a long time until later that night when I offered *pyebaek.*[15] Exhausted and tense, I was fatigued to the point of speechlessness. My husband was the eldest son of a family with three sons and two daughters. I was just a clueless fourteen-year-old bride who had become the eldest daughter-in-law. The youngest of my husband's younger siblings was a baby not even a hundred days old.

The bridal room was a cramped space created by placing a chest of drawers on the upper side of the main room—barely enough space for two people to lie down. My mother-in-law slept with her two daughters and her newborn son on the lower side of the room. Regardless of how much effort was made to keep the fire going, the upper side remained frigid. I cocooned myself in layers and secured a belt around my waist before going to bed. One day, my husband asked why I wore clothes to bed. Whenever I noticed any change in him, I pretended to be sick. After that, my mother-in-law sent my husband to the room reserved for the men of the house, and the upper space became mine.

My mother-in-law was ill-natured and malicious. Whenever I cooked, she barked, "I brought in someone who can't even cook a decent meal," and heaped curses on me with acrimony. I went out to the field and weeded, even on scorching hot days when others in the household napped during lunch break. I would make do with just three or four spoonfuls of food for lunch, gulping down some

---

15. 폐백, traditional ceremony held by a newly-wedded couple after their wedding, to pay respect to the groom's family.

salty *doenjang* and filling the rest of my stomach with water before heading back to the fields.

My mother-in-law's abuse grew worse day by day. She refused to feed me properly, sparingly ladling rice into my tiny metal bowl. It was nowhere near enough to fill my stomach, drained from grueling housework and fieldwork. My father-in-law was aware of this, so he left some rice in his bowl after a meal, pouring water into the bowl and covering the lid as if he had finished eating. I would eat his leftovers in the kitchen, out of sight of my mother-in-law. But soon enough, she caught onto this scheme. One day, cross with me, she poured the leftover watery rice into the dog's bowl. When no one was looking, I scooped it up from the dog's bowl with my bare hands and ate it.

I was always famished but couldn't show it because I feared my mother-in-law. My mind was consumed by thoughts of my hunger, fear, and exhaustion, leaving no space for anything else. Red bedbugs infested my room, and lice gnawed on my head. I could feel the grainy bedbugs when I rubbed my forearm in my sleep. Still, I didn't mind being bitten by bedbugs because I was so deep in sleep.

When the rainy season prevented me from going out to work in the fields, I spent more time with my mother-in-law. She removed frayed and mismatched socks from the chest and told me to patch them. She rolled up hemp and cotton pants, skirts, and new sock fabric and threw them at me.

Not long after I was married, my mother-in-law handed me the fabric that had been tied to the palanquin and asked me to make her a *jeogori*. After much thought and effort, I managed to make it, but I must have sewn the lining incorrectly. I was quite frightened and kept an eye on my mother-in-law as she ripped the *jeogori* apart and threw it my way, yelling at me to make it again.

"This damned miscreant! Did you grow up pampered and coddled? You can't even sew properly!"

I was so intimidated that I couldn't even look my mother-in-law in the face, let alone ask her about anything I didn't know. Even as I was running in and out of the house, working all day, I was consumed with anxiety about how I was to live. When the sun went down, and I lay down to sleep, all I could think about was my parents and younger siblings.

Once the rainy season passed, my mother-in-law again drove me out to the fields each day after breakfast, instructing, "Go weed!"

After the rainy season, the field was like a sweat lodge. By midday, steam rose from the ground, and the scorching sun beat down from the sky. In the bean field, bristly crabgrass grew so vigorously that the sprouts of beans were barely visible. It was extremely strenuous to pluck the crabgrass by hand because of its tough roots. My palms were shredded to the point of bleeding.

Hot steam rose when I sat in the field's furrows, making it difficult to breathe, but strangely, my heart was at ease. There, I didn't have to endure being cursed at or beaten. Then, as the sun began to set and the wind blew, my mother-in-law arrived with a hoe.

"Where are you? Go work the rice paddy."

This time, she sent me to the rice fields to weed. Weeding in the paddy field was even harder because I had to bend over the whole time. The paddies were filled with leeches that bit maliciously at my legs, scaring me. When I lifted my legs after weeding, I found them covered in black leeches clinging to my skin. The sight was so terrifying and revolting that I would slap them with my hands, and blood would flow from where they fell off.

The summer sun was relentless. A few spoonfuls of rice were digested in no time. At times like this, it felt like the sky and the earth were spinning wildly around me, that I would collapse at any moment.

Whenever I had a spare moment, after all the weeding and washing, my mother-in-law sent me to the shore. In the winter, I would dig through frosted mud to catch octopuses and pick green laver from the rocks there. Once, I lost consciousness in the tidal flats on a freezing winter day. Fortunately, someone from a neighboring village happened to pass by and found me. He was said to live in a haunted house—he carried me there, laying me down near the furnace and reviving me by pouring hot water over me.

During the summer, I caught clams from the mud flats. One evening, my mother-in-law ordered me to peel the clams while she rolled wheat flour to make *kalguksu* (wheat noodles) and *mil-bandaegi* (round, flat flour cake). I went to the well in the yard and started shucking them. Although the sun had set, the evening seemed endless. I thought of home.

"*Yaaa!*" Once again, my mother-in-law's shouts thundered like a lightning bolt.

"That cursed bad seed, acting all plaintive and pitiable..."

My mother-in-law came out of the kitchen screaming, threw the clay bowl full of clams over my head, and then started punching me. The pungent smell of the clams and the burning punches threw me into a daze.

"I am sorry! I am sorry..."

I didn't even have time to think about what I had done wrong. I just kept begging for mercy. My mother-in-law's beatings were indiscriminate. She would swing at me with whatever she could get her hands on: a wooden poker, a rake to draw out ashes, a broom, or a ladle. Whenever she got angry, she would beat and scratch me viciously.

Still, it was easier to bear the agony of my physical body than the aching of my heart from unbearable yearning. When I woke up at dawn, I missed my mother to the point of feeling like I was dying. When the sun went down, and darkness loomed, I missed her even more and would choke up with tears, feeling as though I were on the brink of madness. I disliked both evenings and mornings. It was easier to endure the long, interminable days when there was barely any time to rest. In the village of Small Boulder, there was a home where another daughter-in-law had been beaten to death. I kept having ominous feelings. It felt like I, too, may die like that.

A Village Swept by an Epidemic

Almost a year after being married, I was finally able to visit my parents' home. My in-laws allowed me to travel only after the autumn farm work was completed and all the crops had been harvested. I packed a huge rice cake into a wicker trunk and sent it home with a porter. At that time, it was customary for the whole village to share a large rice cake of *jeolpyeon*[16] and *injeolmi*.[17] I visited every house in my village, passing out rice cakes and greeting the villagers. My hometown was small, with only thirteen sparsely populated households. Compared to my husband's village, it was humble.

In one home, I was warmly welcomed with a bowl of sweet rice drink. It was so delicious. But when I came home and boasted about it, my mother was concerned.

---

16. 절편, a patterned rice cake.

17. 인절미, a rice cake coated with sweet bean flour.

"There's a person in that house with an infectious disease," she told me.

Only then did I remember that the woman served me the rice drink from her nephew's bowl—her nephew, a typhoid patient. I wasn't too worried. No matter the severity of the contagious disease, I did not believe anything bad would happen from one bowl of a sweet drink. But as night fell, I began to feel strange, so cold and shaky that I couldn't even think straight. My mother's fears undoubtedly came true.

As I fell ill, my family members also began succumbing to the disease, one by one. My mother collapsed, and my siblings were bedridden. It was beyond our means to obtain any medicine. In 1944, towards the end of World War II, we were beyond destitute and barely survived on the grain we had harvested and crushed into a paste in a mortar for our meals. My sister's father-in-law collected pine branches for us to use as firewood, rolling them into our yard without entering. Homes infected with typhoid fever hung straw ropes on the front gate and left a large clay pot on the other side of the door. Neighbors would draw water and fill the pot for the family to use for drinking and cooking.

I was sick all winter, ill through the new year and as I turned sixteen. I could not return to my married home. My hair fell out due to typhoid fever, and my body was so emaciated that I looked ghastly.

My family cycled through bouts of illness. After a month or two of the disease, I would recover only to fall ill again, and my younger siblings also took turns suffering. We went through this cycle of illness and recovery repeatedly.

Since we'd eaten all the grain through the winter, barely anything was left to eat. Hunger was as unbearable as typhoid fever. As our illness continued, all we had left was a gourd of soybeans, which we roasted and boiled before adding more water and drinking it as a meal. My six-year-old younger brother Jong-Yeon complained that his stomach ached whenever he opened his eyes.

"*Nuna*, my stomach hurts. I can't live with this stomachache. Let's please go beg for some food."

My little brother, who did not know how to adequately express his hunger and pain, clutched his stomach and sobbed loudly. It was heartbreaking to see Jong-Yeon with his big eyes and a body as skinny as a tree branch from starvation.

Jong-Yeon often clutched his stomach and cried out in pain several times a day. To trick his mouth, I would add sliced cucumber to the water and make a watery soup to feed him. But the fullness only lasted until he peed.

One day, my famished little brother, who used to plead with me to beg for food, died in his sleep without ever setting foot in a hospital. We had heard it was good to boil poppy stems to feed a child with dysentery colic, and he drank the water and fell asleep, never to wake up again. I wondered, since he passed away in his sleep, could he have forgotten his hunger for at least a moment?

Jong-Yeon wasn't the only one to succumb to the illness. The typhoid outbreak was terrifying enough to claim the lives of sixteen people in a village of thirteen homes.

Thus, over the course of a few years, my mother had to bid farewell to three family members under her care, including my father, who, determined to feed his family, had died from a combination of overwork and cirrhosis of the liver a few years before while trying to clear a barely arable gravel field beyond the hills. Too destitute to obtain medicine, we heard that mugwort and melon stems could be used medicinally. I tore the mugwort and melon stems to pieces, ground them, and gave them to my father, praying as he consumed the herbal remedy, but it was all in vain.

Throughout that season of typhoid, even when I was so sick

that I fell in and out of consciousness, I was still haunted by my terrifying mother-in-law in my dreams.

I must run away. I can't ever live with my in-laws again, I thought to myself.

Over and over again, in my dreams, I promised myself that I would not live in my mother-in-law's home again. But after ten months, I was well enough that my maternal grandmother insisted it was time for me to return. It was only thanks to typhoid fever that I had been able to stay at my family's house for such a lengthy period in the first place. The journey back was as dreadful as ever, and my footsteps were heavy.

When I returned to my husband's house, nothing had changed. My husband, who had barely acknowledged me before my disappearance, was in the yard when I arrived but offered no response to my return. My mother-in-law acted as if I were invisible and didn't say a word to me. They didn't even acknowledge the presence of my maternal grandmother, who had accompanied me there. She sat alone for a long time, looking abashed, before finally leaving without being greeted.

I returned to the fields to weed and suffered under my mother-in-law's abuse. One day, as I was weeding, an airplane flew high overhead. Korea had been liberated. The Japanese, who had taken away our language and family-given names and plundered our grains, had finally returned to their own country—but nothing had changed for me.

Then, one day, deep into autumn, things finally reached a breaking point. I was up at dawn, starting a fire under the cauldron, when my mother-in-law came into the kitchen and began striking me furiously with a wooden poker. I escaped to the yard, having been savagely beaten without knowing why. My mother-in-law flew into the yard, grabbed a wooden pole standing by the cowshed, and swung it at me. The blow hit my thigh, and it hurt badly.

"This cursed seed is badmouthing her husband's family all over town."

When my father-in-law tried to stop her, my mother-in-law swung the yard broom at him as well. That day, as soon as I finished the morning dishes, I ran out of the house and dashed to my family's home, just over a mountain. Having lost any shred of warmth towards my in-laws, I had no reason to hesitate.

When I entered my maternal grandmother's house, tears poured out. But my grandmother and the rest of the family told me to go back at once.

"Whether you die or live, you will be the Oh family's ghost," they said.

This time, my *hyeongbu*[18] took me back to my husband's home. But I turned right around and ran back to my family's house again. Next time, my uncle took me back. He even went as far as to entrust me directly to my mother-in-law, saying, "Please take good care of this immature girl."

In the time it took me to run away and be forced to return twice, the sun had set, and evening had arrived. My heart was no longer in Small Boulder. While doing the evening dishes, I overheard my mother-in-law talking to my husband through the open floor between the rooms.

"I'm going to Seok-Ho's house to discuss something," my mother-in-law said. "In the meantime, break up the chestnut branches into rods and leave the hemp rope hanging on the pole in front of the room. Bitches who run away must be punished by having their legs twisted."

Seok-Ho's? I thought. *Wasn't Seok-Ho the family who beat their daughter-in-law to death…?*

A chill ran from the nape of my neck to my spine.

---

18. 형부, an older sister's husband.

It seemed they would kill me. Why else would they need the rope?

My husband stood silently for a long while before disappearing. I finished washing the dishes, restless with anxiety. I couldn't go inside. Finding me pacing the yard, my father-in-law tried to soothe me.

"My child, there's no way a tiger would eat her own cub, no matter how much she hates it. Go inside and sit for a while. If I hear any sounds of beating, I'll come put a stop to it," he said.

But my frightened heart would not calm down. I couldn't even speak properly. As dusk fell and darkness crept in, I became even more anxious. I occupied myself with needless tasks, replacing the water in a pot where I had put ground acorns to soak. While fetching and replacing the water, I only thought of my escape.

Inside, my father-in-law kept his door open and smoked a long pipe, keeping his eyes on me the whole time. There was nothing I could do. My stomach ached terribly from the tension. Finally, I entered the outhouse in the yard and peered through the straw wall. I heard the sound of my father-in-law knocking the ash from his pipe. It seemed like he was watching for signs of me in the outhouse.

How could I escape? Where could I flee to?

I noticed a hole under the back fence made of reeds and bush clover. Without further thought, I flew from the outhouse, crawling on my stomach through the hole and ran off in a frenzy. I raced along a mountain path shrouded in night fog so thick I could not see ahead.

That was the last time I returned to my family's home. I never went back to the village where my vicious mother-in-law lived.

SIX

Destined to Wear
a Purple Cloth

Unlike nowadays, when I was young, there were many diseases that people didn't know the causes of. When I was about five-years-old, my younger brother, Joong-Hyun, was struck ill with a mysterious fever. The rumor was that it all started after a Japanese police officer supervising village road workers had opened the door to a room where a baby was sleeping. Maybe it was really a case of bad luck when his forehead swelled up to the size of a fist, and he drew close to death. For Joong-Hyun, my family called for a *gut*—a Shamanic ritual performed right in our courtyard in the presence of the whole village. My maternal grandmother, a famous *manshin*, performed the *gut*, and our yard was overcrowded with people watching with no room to move. Fortunately, thanks to my grandmother's devoted ritual, my brother recovered.

A *Byeong-gut*[19] was also performed for the family of a male *manshin*. The shaman's father had been unable to move for

---

19. 병굿, an illness ritual.

several months, his joints paralyzed. The villagers gathered in a circle, bowed, and prayed for his fast recovery. The *gut* had been performed and offerings given at a nearby mountain, and later, it was said that an enormous pair of snakes appeared and sat coiled on a boulder during the ritual before disappearing under a rock. After the ritual, when the father regained the use of his legs, the villagers whispered among themselves that he had been punished for offending the gods by getting drunk where his son served his gods as a shaman.

Nowadays, people scorn *mudangs* and *guts* as superstitions, but in the past, everyone relied on Shamanic practices and spirits, worshipping them at home. They believed that *Samshin*[20] occupied the rooms of a home, *Seongjushin*[21] the courtyard, *Jowangshin*[22] the kitchen, and *Eopshin*[23] the shed. It was even believed that the outhouse was occupied by *Chikshin*,[24] ensuring that people did not speak or behave improperly anywhere.

I was incredibly sickly when I was young, suffering almost daily from illnesses like stomachaches caused by roundworms, malaria, and other common ailments. My maternal grandfather would pluck some *minari* and shove it into a rat hole facing east before making me shout three times while holding my breath.

---

20. 삼신, the Triple Goddess of fertility, childbirth, mothers, newborns, and children under seven-years-old.

21. 성주신, the Household God who protects the household, believed to be the male leader of a household's gods and goddesses.

22. 조왕신, the Goddess of the Hearth and Kitchen, who watches over the fire and water of the home.

23. 업신, a deity that protects the belongings and money of the home, sometimes taking the form of a snake.

24. 칙신, the Outhouse or Bathroom Goddess who brings illness when family members misbehave or cross her.

"Malaria blows in! The whole way in!" we chanted. "Malaria air is going in! How dare it make people sick? Cast all the malaria and sick air into the rat hole!"

When we performed this around sunrise, unbelievably, I wouldn't get sick for three whole days. Still, in late spring and fall, I suffered from malaria again and again. Adults believed a patient's body had to stay uncomfortable to scare the disease away and wouldn't let me lie down. But at times, I would escape, collapsing and passing out wherever I landed.

Once, when he was still alive, my father led a bull out of the barn, then placed a straw mat in the yard and told me to lie down on it. Then he covered me with straw and drove the bull toward me, clicking his tongue, "Tsk, tsk, tsk."

"A living person is lying here, so don't step on her. Step over her. Begone, malaria!" he said.

I was stiff with fear the whole time. But then, as if it knew I was lying under the bed of straw, the bull would step over me.

Afterward, the straw was lifted from my body and burned while the adults shouted, "Scram, damned malaria, go to the ends of the earth!"

Again, I seemed to get better for a few days, only to soon fall sick once more. My body shivered, and my head ached so badly that even after sleeping for a long time, I would awaken only to fall right back to sleep. When I closed my eyes, I heard the sound of rattles and bells jingling and saw menacing-looking people descending from the sky on red horses. Sometimes, those people rode tigers and rushed right toward me, screaming. Frightened, I woke up. While dreaming, I couldn't tell whether my eyes were closed or open, could not distinguish between being asleep or awake. It seemed that right before my eyes, people dressed in military regalia descended from the clouds in succession. In this trancelike dream state, I sometimes flew among them. When I managed to wake up from a dream, my whole body was drenched in sweat, and I was terribly scared. The next time I had the same dream, I would repeat to myself, "This is just a dream." Then I would mingle and play with the people in my dreams, ride clouds and cross streams in a Milky Way mist, and traverse completely different worlds. When I awakened after wholeheartedly playing in my dream, my head stopped aching, and my heart felt more at ease.

If I sensed someone calling me in the mornings, I hastily dressed and went outside. Then I ran like an arrow towards the shallow well next to the kitchen, where people drew water with a gourd. It felt like someone was trying to talk to me from the well. So I talked back while looking at my reflection in the water.

"Hey, why are you there?"

"I'm going to follow you!"

After conversing with myself, asking and answering questions alone, I felt my mind clear—lighter as I lifted my shoulders, as though ready to fly away at any moment. As I looked up at the sky and down into the well, misty steam billowed, making it difficult to see through the clear well water. I babbled as I peered into the well. Watching me like this, my father's heart probably burned into a rock of black charcoal.

One day, while my mother lit a fire in the kitchen, my father spoke to her.

"That Neomse," he began. "If we had let her die when she was born, we would have been spared heartache. What absurdity we are made to witness. I know it's sinful to say, but if she can't be a decent human being, she might as well die …"

Then my father would sigh heavily and smoke a cigarette.

The grandmother at the male shaman's home sometimes ran to our house when her son got drunk and caused trouble. On the nights she slept over, the sound of ten *janggu*[25] drums lingered in my ears, and no matter how much I plugged them, the drumbeat would not go away. I had no choice but to keep up with the rhythm with my mouth, jumping wildly to the beat and dancing frenziedly.

Sometimes, while lighting the cooking fire in the kitchen, I suddenly felt the urge to dance. Since we were too poor to afford firewood, we piled dry grass in the kitchen for kindling. I quickly stuffed a pile of grass into the stove and danced alone until it burned up, jumping up and down, clanging and clashing pot lids. As I danced, the fire in the stove burned out, leaving only pitch-black ash. By the time I put more grass in, my body felt as light as a feather.

If dancing alone did not make my body feel lighter, I would sneak into my grandmother's room, take down her scarlet *Daeshinbal*,[26] and carry it all over her room, running around frenetically. Looking back now, it seems like I was attempting to heal the *mubyeong*[27] that visited my body.

But once I passed the age of sixteen, I could no longer manage the spirit sickness on my own.

At seventeen, I fell severely ill once again. An elderly village man who read sacred sutras came to see me. It is said that since ancient times, elders would drive out evil spirits by reciting the *Okchugyeong*.[28] But during his visit, the elderly man stopped reading the sutras and shook his head.

"It doesn't look like it will work. The only way she will recover is by using a purple cloth."

---

25. 장구, an hourglass shaped drum that is most representative in traditional Korean music.

26. 대신발, a Shamanic sash or flag used in rituals to invoke gods and ancestors.

27. 무병/신병, also called *shinbyeong*, the Shamanic sickness, spirit sickness.

28. 경, a Taoist sacred text often read or recited by a blind person.

The purple cloth was the headscarf worn by the *mudangs* of Hwanghae Province during a *gut*. This meant that I was suffering from *shinbyeong* to become a shaman. My family members didn't know what to do. Having seen my maternal grandmother's struggles as a shaman, they were well aware of the hardships and suffering that being a shaman entailed. They were determined to find a way to prevent me from becoming a shaman myself.

* * *

It was the night of the full moon. My family suggested we perform a *dalmaji*,[29] greeting the moon and praying to *Ilweolseong-shin*.[30] We cut a long bundle of straw and tied them into knots according to my age, making a moon-greeting pole. With the pole in hand, we crossed the stream and climbed the low hill near the rice field. As the full moon rose right before my eyes, an aunt instructed me to kneel and bow. I bowed as many times as my age. Then, my aunt set fire to the moon pole I held. As the straw crackled and burned, I bowed incessantly and prayed earnestly to the moon to heal my sick body. At the same time, I felt a strange desire to become a shaman if it meant my illness would be cured. Perhaps I was just so worn out from the constant loneliness and pain of my life. If it meant that something could change, I was willing to embrace the challenging journey of becoming a shaman.

Did the Celestial god read my thoughts? As I laid down the

---

29. 달맞이, a full moon tradition that takes place especially on the Grand Full Moon (*Daeboreum*, 대보름) or the Harvest Full Moon (*Chuseok*, 추석), when people go outside to greet and pray to the rising moon.

30. 일월성신, the Celestial God of the Sun, Moon, and Stars.

burnt moon pole and jumped over it, a shower of dazzling white stars suddenly poured from the sky. I feared I would get seriously hurt if hit by the stars, so I ran wildly toward the creek. Just as I was about to cross the stream, though I didn't trip on anything, I fell over and lost consciousness. That is when the gods descended on my body.

SEVEN

My Maternal Grandmother, Kim Cheon-il

My maternal grandmother was a renowned great shaman, known not only in the Ongjin area but also in distant towns dozens of *li* away. Her Shamanic gifts were profound and highly regarded, and her names, *Cheon-il-i Manshin* and *Batubogi Manshin*, were famous even among those who didn't know her personally. When she performed a *gut*, many people from faraway towns came to watch.

When my younger brother Joong-Hyun was ill, and my maternal grandmother, who lived in Ongjin at the time, came to our village to hold a *gut*, our small yard was overflowing with people. Even people who lived on the other side of the mountain flocked to see my grandmother's *gut*. While some just wanted to see the famous *manshin's* face, some men showed up hoping to have drinks and possibly more with her. As if!

Such ridiculousness did not work on my grandmother. She harshly rebuked such men, saying, "The absurdity I must endure!

How dare you ask me when you can go home and ask your wife instead? While I've been given the bitter fate of becoming a shaman, I'm not someone you can treat disrespectfully! If you're here to see a *gut*, just watch it quietly instead of spewing bullshit."

After her harsh scolding, people didn't dare make further advances toward her. Her temperament was notorious for being stubborn and unyielding. She had a reputation as a *yangban*[31] *manshin* in Ongjin, and most people were too afraid to speak to her.

My maternal grandmother was born into the Cheongpoong Kim family and married my grandfather, who is of the Jeon-ju Lee[32] family, giving birth to two daughters. In order to have a son, she went to the village shrine and the mountains to pray. It was then that spirits descended on her body, and she ended up becoming a *mudang* instead. My grandfather strongly opposed my grandmother becoming a shaman, unable to accept that a woman of aristocratic lineage might be destined for such a fate. My grandfather purchased *kyeongmyeonjusa*,[33] wrote *bujeok*,[34] and hid them in her clothes and pillows. Despite his efforts, my grandmother found and destroyed all of them.

That wasn't all. My grandmother often disappeared without a word. After searching for her over an entire day, my grandfather would eventually find her dancing frantically at a *gut* she'd

31. 양반, a noble and aristocratic class from Joseon era.

32. 전주이씨, a surname that originates from Jeonju City of the Jeolla Province; also, a noble surname that was held by the royal family of the Joseon Dynasty and the imperial family.

33. 경면주사, a natural mineral crystal with a cinnabar or reddish-brown color, which contains mercury sulfide as its main component. It is sometimes used as medicine in traditional Korean medicine.

34. 부적, a talisman with red writing or drawings, used to ward off evil spirits and prevent disasters.

discovered, sometimes dozens of *li* away. My grandfather would stand by for the entire *gut* and then send someone to draw my grandmother out deep in the forest or to another secluded place. There, he would grab her and tear at her flesh, mercilessly beating her with ash tree branches, leaving her body black and blue. If she didn't yield to his violence, he would take out the pocketknife he carried and hold it against her neck threateningly. In this way, my grandfather did everything he could to suppress her spirit energy.

However, there was no way to stop my grandmother, who had already been called by the spirits. Despite being bruised and unable to walk properly from being beaten, she would go out searching for a *gut*. Her broken and battered body would miraculously recover whenever she danced at these rituals.

One day, enraged, my grandfather dragged my grandmother into the house by her hair. My mother and aunt, just young girls, paced around the yard helplessly. Shortly after, my grandmother's screams were heard from inside.

"*Aigoo*, it's hot! *Aigoo*, I'm going to die!"

My mother and aunt opened the door and stopped dead in their tracks, horrified. The room was hazy with smoke and the smell of burning flesh as their father used metal pokers and irons from the fiery brazier to brand their mother's thighs, mercilessly burning and searing her flesh. My mother and aunt clutched my grandfather and tried to stop him, to no avail.

My grandmother's face blanched as she screamed breathlessly, "*Aigoo*, it's burning! *Aigoo*, you're killing me!"

How long did this excruciating horror last? At some point, the pain disappeared from my grandmother's face. She even went as far as to open her clothes to give her flesh to her husband and said, "*Aigoo*, how cool! *Aigoo*, how refreshing! Go ahead and burn and sear me here and there, too!"

My grandfather became angrier and started to deeply scorch my grandmother's tender flesh with the hot iron. As pieces of her flesh melted off, my terrified mother and aunt held on to each other, crying and screaming for my grandfather to stop. Meanwhile, my grandmother kept saying, "*Aigoo*, how cool. *Aigoo*, how refreshing," pressing herself against the hot iron. After a while, my grandfather shook his head.

"*Ai!* You cursed, wicked thing!"

There was no way to quell the intensifying spirit energy rising in my grandmother. Soon, she ran away to another town to escape my grandfather. There, she met a good spirit mother and soon gained a great reputation as a *manshin* herself. After she left my grandfather, he briefly lived with another wife, but problems plagued him. As a merchant, whenever he traveled by donkey, its leg would break repeatedly. His second wife was so vicious towards my mother, as the daughter of his first wife, that household elders and neighbors persuaded him to ask my grandmother to return to him. My grandfather, regretting his prior actions, sent word for my grandmother. Meanwhile, my grandmother had risen to such prominence that when she returned to her hometown, she brought three large carts full of various Shamanic tools and valuables.

Visitors never ceased arriving at my spiritually-gifted grandmother's home. During the Lunar New Year, the narrow road to her house became congested with people coming to see her for a reading. Elderly women from all around appeared with bundles of rice, which they strapped to their backs with straw ropes to present as an offering to my grandmother.

There was a small stream in front of my grandmother's house, and during their visits, the old women—those who became my grandmother's "regulars"—would cross the stream with their walking sticks, dressed in white *sobok*.[35] Even in the dead of winter, they came across the stream barefoot, carrying their socks and straw shoes to keep them dry. I still vividly remember the procession of elderly ladies dressed in white filling the narrow path like a white ribbon.

But above all, what captivated my heart was the divination table my grandmother kept in the main room. Whenever I was called to run errands, I would see that my grandmother had laid out a white *bojagi* cloth on the table and placed rice on top of it. I was fascinated by the way she spread out the grains of rice to read them. As I was transfixed, staring at her, my grandmother would suddenly shout, "Neomse-*ya*! What are you staring at? Leave immediately!" I instantly snapped out of my trance.

My grandfather still opposed my grandmother's Shamanic practices, and bizarre things happened all the time in their home. Almost every day after my maternal grandmother returned to the house, a tiger would come down from the mountains and shake the front gate. All night long, the sound of cats meowing and dogs barking did not stop, and there were countless tiger claw marks on the front gate. On snowy mornings, you could see the enormous tiger footprints left in the snow around the house overnight.

One foggy, rainy day, my grandfather was returning home from the marketplace. He had stopped by his friend's house to obtain a *sapsal*[36] dog. As he turned onto a secluded path, my grandfather heard a sound like whistling wind, and when he looked around to see what it was, he saw a tiger sitting about five meters ahead of him on the path. My grandfather quickly hid the puppy inside his robe and kept walking. As he did, the tiger

---

35. 소복, all-white women's *hanbok*.

36. 삽살개, a native dog breed in Korea with long history, known for its shaggy hair.

stood and walked on, maintaining his distance as my grandfather approached. My grandfather and the tiger walked like that for about *ten li*[37] until they finally reached the village. When my grandfather arrived in front of his home, he let out a sigh of relief and released the puppy from his robe. He was about to remove his sweat-drenched clothes when he suddenly heard the dog yelp. Turning around, he saw the tiger snatch the puppy he had just sat down and take off.

Another time, while returning from a village beyond the hill, a tiger followed, sometimes leading and sometimes trailing behind. The lights from its blue eyes were bright enough to illuminate the path. When they reached the entrance to the village, my grandfather shouted to warn the villagers that a tiger was approaching.

"A neighborhood guest is making an entrance! Treat the guest generously!"

As soon as he shouted, the tiger suddenly growled. They were standing in front of a house that kept a large male guard dog, and all at once, the tiger disappeared with the dog in its mouth. Seeing this, my grandfather opened his mouth in disbelief, but his voice went hoarse.

"My goodness, the craziness I've seen!" he murmured to himself inwardly.

I can't believe I was followed by a fierce mountain tiger roaming for its prey. Did it suddenly snatch Kwangsu's dog? If that dog hadn't been there, it could have been me instead.

Upon returning home, my grandfather was bedridden for several days. The village grandmothers were terrified of him and found him difficult to deal with—known locally as 'Old Beomchi' after a type of fish that attacks people and 'Old Rockfish,' given because of his scary, reddish, bulging, rough exterior—so

---

37. 십리, approximately 5 kilometers or 3.1 miles.

when they came to visit, they whispered to each other, "Is Old Rockfish around?"

One day, there was a *gut* at my grandmother's home. My grandfather refused to leave his room, saying he didn't want to see it. But a strange thing happened when my grandmother, embodied with *Janggun-shin*,[38] jumped onto the *jakdu*[39] knife blades! Her feet stuck to the blades, and she couldn't move an inch. People had never seen anything like it before and suspected it was caused by Old Rockfish's foul temper. My grandmother tried hard to separate her feet from the blades, but no matter how much she sweated and used all her strength, they remained stuck on the knives. Eventually, people barged into my grandfather's room and dragged him out. They scolded him severely, saying that the gods were enraged that a person in a *mudang's* household would be so contemptuous and disrespectful towards the spirits. They ordered him to bow before the blades until the gods were appeased and their wrath abated, but my grandfather refused.

"Only a son of a bitch bows to his own wife!"

My grandfather roared as he grabbed my grandmother and hoisted her up from the *jakdu*. The blades flew off the frame, still attached to my grandmother's feet. Startled, the village elders rushed to support them from both sides. Only then did my grandfather release her, and she found herself released from the blades. After being freed from the *jakdu*, my grandmother collapsed on the straw mat, weeping and using the edge of her garment to wipe her tears. My mother cried alongside her.

After that, stubborn Old Rockfish began to gradually

---

38. 장군신, the Warrior General God.

39. 작두, a traditional cutting tool with one or two large blades on a wooden frame, used to cut straw, grass, and herbs. During a Shamanic *gut*, a shaman embodying the Warrior God will jump and dance on the sharp blades without any injury.

understand and appreciate my grandmother's spiritual world. Sometimes, he would even help write down scheduled *gut* dates and visitors' birth dates for divination. Still, he fell ill toward the end of his life, and his condition worsened over time. Amid a scorching August, just before he passed, he motioned for my grandmother.

Sitting by his side, my mother wept and said, "Father, it's better that Mother does not see you go, so she's gone out."

The way my mother clenched her teeth to contain her tears made a strong impression on me. Still, I went outside, feeling I had to summon my grandmother as my grandfather had asked. Grandmother was crying bitterly, plucking sesame seeds from their pods. When she saw me, she asked if my grandfather had passed, wiping her tear-strewn and snot-stained face with the corner of her skirt. I just shook my head, turned my face away, and stared at a distant mountain for a while, tears pouring down my face.

"Grandmother, Grandfather is gesturing for you. Come, please? You must come quickly to see him go."

"You should go. I cannot witness your grandfather's passing," my grandmother said as she burst into tears again.

At that time, I was too young to understand my grandmother's heart. When my father passed away, we had stayed by his side until the end.

My mother stood by my father when he passed, so why can't my grandmother see my grandfather's passing? I wondered to myself.

When I returned to the room where my grandfather lay, my mother was speaking softly to him. She told him that she had sent a telegram to her sister in Haeju and that she would be arriving soon. After positioning my grandfather's head towards the doorway, my mother spread a long piece of white hemp cloth on the floor and placed money on it for his journey to the afterlife. She also placed money in both of his hands.

Then, in a strained and tearful voice, she said, "Father! Don't worry about Mother or us. Please go comfortably. Don't cling to this world anymore. Enter into the bliss of paradise."

My mother wiped away her tears and gently closed her father's eyes. A moment later, his neck tilted weakly to one side. My mother kept us from crying aloud. It was believed that if people wailed too soon before the *chohon*[40] was sung, it would distract the *jeoseungsaja*[41] from leading the deceased away.

Mother prepared the offering for the *jeoseungsaja* and laid out three bowls of rice, three plates of *namul*,[42] three cups of liquor, and three pairs of straw shoes, placing them outside the front gate and hanging grandfather's clothes on the door. After reciting three verses of *chohon*, she finally untied her hair and began to wail. The sound of her sorrowful lamenting was heart-wrenching.

Despite their challenging early years, my grandfather had become my mother's only source of comfort and strength, as she had witnessed her own mother's difficult life as a shaman. His passing probably felt like the collapse of her world. Even now, the memory of my mother gently patting grandfather's coffin and murmuring, "I wish you waited to leave me until after the children grew a bit more," breaks my heart.

---

40. 초혼, the ritual act of calling forth the name of the deceased person.

41. 저승사자, the guide of death who escorts the soul of a deceased person to the Afterlife.

42. 나물, various cooked edible greens and vegetables. Three colors: white, brown, and green are commonly used in rituals.

EIGHT

I've Come on a Lonely Path, I've Come to Bless

The summer I was seventeen-years-old, I underwent a *Naerim-gut*[43] to become a *mudang* under the guidance of my maternal grandmother, who became my spirit mother. She spread the news to her regular clients, and many people prepared grains and alcohol for the ritual. Since my *malmun*[44] had opened, allowing me to communicate with spirits and convey their messages to others, I undertook a *geollip*,[45] traveling through the village gathering

---

43. 내림굿, an initiation ritual to receive and acknowledge the Shamanic gods that have descended.

44. 말문, the doorway of divine words, opened when a shaman-to-be starts communicating with her gods, channeling them, providing divination to people.

45. 걸립/건립, the rite of passage where a shaman-to-be goes around the village announcing the upcoming *Naerim-gut*, giving divination readings, and collecting donations of money, grain, and metals that will be used to prepare the initiation ritual.

rice and metal for the ritual. For *gangshinmu*[46] *mudangs*, even the process of preparing to receive the Shamanic tools was not easy. At that time, it was customary for a *mudang* to collect scrap metal from throughout the village and use it to have their tools crafted, rather than simply ordering *jakdu* or bells from a blacksmith, as is done now.

During the first Lunar month of the year I turned seventeen, I went through my first *geollip* and collected scrap metal from the village. After that month's full moon, the spirits descended on my body while I was out beneath the moon, trying to heal my spirit sickness. Since then, I constantly felt like my body was floating and couldn't stay still, with an insatiable urge to wander. I recall that it was around the eighteenth day of the month when I started the *geollip*, collecting metal.

During that time, I was living with my aunt and uncle in Pansidong. One day, my aunt and I went to the creek together to do laundry. Washing clothes before the full moon of the first Lunar month was taboo, so the large wooden bucket was piled high with laundry. The two of us barely lifted the wooden bucket and placed it on our heads. Staggering under its weight, I suddenly lifted it from my head and placed it on the ground all by myself. The laundry seemed insignificant at that moment. Something was pulling me from afar, and my body felt weightless, making it unbearable.

"Let's go! Let's go quickly!" I mumbled.

With those words, I started running wildly, not even noticing that my straw shoes had come off. I ran across the rice paddies and field banks until I reached the village. There, I began entering any house I felt led to.

---

46. 강신무, a *mudang* who becomes such through the descent of and possession by spirits or gods as opposed to *seseupmu* (세습무), the hereditary *mudangs* who learn the arts of the *gut* as passed down in their family.

"I've come on a lonely path; I've come to bless.
I've come to open closed doors.
Like snow fluttering on a high mountain
and ashes blowing on a low mountain,
As this family rises up and that family creeps low,
I've come to gather dead metal and make it alive again."

I spun around and danced wildly. Strangely, this song and chant I had never heard before flowed out of my mouth. After stopping my spinning dance, I stamped my feet on the ground and commanded loudly, "There is a metal crying out in this house that is seventeen- or eighteen-years-old. It's on the shelf, so bring it here right away!"

The homeowner looked bewildered and went into the kitchen. He came out shortly with an old brass rice paddle in his hand, his face filled with surprise.

"Wow, you are truly gifted! How could you have known there was a rice paddle there?"

With his face a mix of surprise and admiration, he readily handed over the brass rice paddle. Receiving a rice paddle in one's first *geollip* was seen as a sign that one was destined to become a great *mudang* whose fortune would expand, so I had a very auspicious beginning.

In another home, I commanded, "There is a seven-year-old bowl in your closet, so bring it to me."

And another, "A crying iron has entered this home, causing illness to the head of the household."

In the old days, it was believed that if impure or blemished metal were brought into a house, it could bring misfortune and illness to the family or livestock. This is why homeowners would readily hand over old brass bowls or spoons as commanded by a new *manshin*.

The more gifted and brilliant a *mudang*, the better she is at locating the hidden metal in every corner of a house and offering accurate divinations. As my *malmun* was opened, I offered various fortunes at each home, such as "Your son will be successful" or "The head of the household will fall on level ground." Where there were disputes, I helped resolve them by discerning true and false.

People hung onto every word I said, finding my predictions amazingly accurate. However, curiously, there were some homes where I couldn't speak a word and felt suffocated and distraught, while in other homes, my words of divination flowed like a river. After pouring out all that was given, my heart felt refreshed, my body felt light, and my footsteps were nimble. No matter how far I had to travel, I didn't feel tired, my body as light as if I were floating on clouds.

In this way, I visited around thirty of the homes that made up the village of Pansidong, gathering metal and rice. Once I'd accumulated a heap of old, worn-out, smooth metal like rice paddles, brass bowls, rice bowls, spoons, and such into my skirt, I went home to empty them into a basket before returning to the village again. On other occasions, a disabled old woman carried a sack and helped me share the heavy load. These elderly women who supported and protected *manshins* were called *Bokjigi*, meaning "a blessing carrier." In front of each home I showed signs of entering, the *Bokjigi* would lead the way and loudly call forth those inside.

"Ahem! A great and powerful new *manshin* has arrived! Open the door quickly!"

The villagers would then come out and greet me warmly.

"Isn't that Neomse? Oh my, you've become a *mudang* now!"

In homes without any brass, they gave rice instead, offering a handful or generously filling a large bowl and saying, "New *manshin*, be blessed and become a great *mudang*."

Once, I suddenly jumped up from sleep to perform a rice *geollip*. As I entered a home and was about to receive rice, the old man of the house came out and asked his wife who I was.

"A new *manshin* has come to collect rice," she replied and tried to hand me a bowl of rice. However, the old man got angry, screaming at me.

"What do you mean collecting rice? Don't utter bullshit. Get the hell out of here!"

Then he started hurling all sorts of vicious curses at me. I couldn't collect any rice and returned home empty-handed. However, three days later, a woman came to our house with a large rice bowl. After placing the offering in front of me, she bowed repeatedly. I was puzzled and just watched in bewilderment. After a while, my grandmother called to me and asked what had happened.

"Neomse, what happened when you went to collect rice at that house?"

I told her what happened. Then my grandmother clicked her tongue pityingly and said, "Apparently, the old man of that house hasn't been able to get up since that day. Go on and pray for him to get up."

The old man rose again only after I prayed with all my heart to Divine Spirit.

Practicing *geollip* was a way to widely announce the arrival of a new *manshin* and build regular relationships with families that would need her support as a shaman. I collected enough metal by wandering around the village, filling a huge basket. I went to the blacksmith to order Shamanic tools: a ninety-nine-bell rattle, a round, hanging *myeongdu*,[47] an *ilweolmyeongdo*,[48] and a *jegeum*,[49] among others, were made. When the molten iron was poured to make the bells, they came out perfectly formed on the first try.

"Nailed it on the first try! Wow, you will become a great *manshin*." The owner of the brass shop was thrilled that the Shamanic tools were made flawlessly on the first attempt. He blessed me, assuring me that I would be very great. Each bell was perfectly shaped and jangled well, and the *myeongdu* came out prettily with its curved center.

Once a fledgling *mudang* attains her Shamanic tools, she is at the threshold of entering a new world, leaving behind her life as a human. By bringing the old, worn-out metal to the divine world of spirits, her tools become anointed with the blessing of being used for good. In its most genuine essence, *geollip* is a sacred ritual for collecting "dead metal" and transforming it into "living metal" through the power of the divine.

---

47. 명두, a mirror that a shaman uses.

48. 일월명도, a Shamanic sword with the sun, moon, and stars engraved on it.

49. 제금, also known as *bara* (바라), a metal percussion instrument resembling cymbals used in a *gut*.

NINE

The Day I Received *Naerim-gut*

When I think of the day I received *Naerim-gut*,[50] tears well up in my eyes, even now. In a poem gifted to me by Do-ol Kim Yong-ok, he wrote:

For what reason did you become a mudang?
A heart calcified in mute suffering,
you couldn't answer if you wanted to

Whenever I see those verses hanging on the wall of my Keumhwa-dang shrine, I ask myself why I became a *mudang*. To others, shamans may appear all-powerful, able to foretell good and bad fortune in human affairs and bless others through prayer, but the reality of our daily lives and what is within our hearts is endlessly wearisome. People burdened with anxieties and suffering

---

50. 내림굿, an initiation ritual to receive and acknowledge the Shamanic gods that have descended.

come to me to relieve their troubles and find comfort, but I myself have nowhere to pour out my own heartaches and loneliness. Sometimes, I find myself shedding lonely tears.

One morning at dawn, the summer I was seventeen, when the world was wet with dewdrops, the wind was blowing gently, and the grains were ripening splendidly in the fields, I dressed in a white *sobok* and climbed the *dangsan*[51] with my maternal grandmother, to welcome the *Sanshin*[52] of Pansidong. My grandmother wrapped me in *soji*[53] paper to cleanse me, then offered a prayer of invocation to the *Sanshin*.

"We have come to receive *Sanshin-nim*. Although she is my precious granddaughter in the human realm, in the realm of the gods, this Neomse is a young and inexperienced daughter of Divine Spirit. I pray that *Sanshin*, filled with great and clear spirit, descends and guides this weak and pitiful soul on the right path."

My grandmother prayed slowly with sincerity. However, before her prayer was over, my body shook vigorously as if it did not belong to me. Strange words poured from my mouth, words that I had never used before, so I could not even understand their meaning. But my grandmother was pleased, slapping her knees. She said that since the sacred flow of words was heard first, I could easily channel gods and spirits.

After descending the mountain and entering the village, I saw from afar that our courtyard was set up for a *gut*. Shamanic gods drawn on hemp paper were hanging all over, and a colorful array

---

51. 당산, a sacred mountain or hill considered holy and worshipped as a guardian deity of a land or village.

52. 산신, the Mountain Spirit.

53. 소지, a wish or prayer paper, the act of burning white paper to cleanse impurity and send wishful prayers to the gods. Also refers to the paper used for such rituals.

of ritual robes and *shinbok*[54] was scattered underneath them. The bright morning sun poured into the courtyard, giving off a feeling of auspiciousness.

In February, I had already undergone the *Heoju-gut*, a ritual that expels evil and false spirits from the body, and had been following *gut* rituals here and there. Even so, I did not fully understand the procedures and meaning of the initiation *gut*. On the day I received the *Naerim-gut*, I could not understand each *geori*[55] that made up the *gut*, so I obediently followed my grandmother's instructions and the lead of other, more experienced shamans. Although I was still inexperienced, I could clearly feel Great Spirit guiding me from within whenever I danced or spoke to people. A young *manshin* kindly explained the *gut's* flow to me in whispers, which helped me keep up.

"Kim Keum-Hwa is receiving *Naerim-gut* today!"

According to our regional traditions, the *gut* began with a *shincheongullim*,[56] invoking spirits and gods for the ritual. It continued with *Sangsanmaji*,[57] welcoming the village's Mountain God, *Bugunim*.[58] *Ilweolseongshinmaji*[59] invited the highest deity

---

54. 신복, god clothing, Shamanic robes representing different gods channeled during *gut*.

55. 거리, the passages of text, song, and dance that comprise the *gut*.

56. 신청울림, a ritual procedure performed at the beginning of any *gut* where the *mudang* announces their intention to perform the *gut* for all the deities. It is a process to call upon the spirits and invite them to descend, and during this procedure, Shamanic instruments are played to beckon the spirits.

57. 상산맞이, welcoming the Mountain God.

58. 부군, the Village Guardian God

59. 일월성신 맞이, welcoming the Celestial God.

in a *mudang's* shrine, and *Mulbaebachigi*[60] was a divination ritual that predicted the future path of the new shaman in honor.

In the yard, I danced with all my heart as the other *manshins* instructed me. Sometimes, when a familiar Shamanic song was performed, I quietly sang along to the chorus. Sometimes, when I danced, my movements became so intense that I could barely endure it. When I lifted my arms and tilted my head, the tips of my hair stood on end as if sucked up into the sky, and I broke out in cold sweat. During the *Mulbaebachigi*, it was said that if enough water droplets rose to drench the end of the hemp cloth, one would become a great and powerful shaman. In my case, water droplets rose from even the outer fabric, causing all who saw it to exclaim in amazement.

Finally, we entered the passage of *Naerim-gut*. A white cloth called *Ilwoldari*[61] was spread from the floor of the home to the end of the courtyard, like a sacred path leading to the world of the spirits. I kneeled at the end of the cloth bridge.

"Lift your head!" As the head shaman in charge of the ritual, my grandmother commanded me loudly and solemnly.

"Lift your head!"

This time, the middle *manshin* conveyed my grandmother's words to me. Throughout the passage of *Naerim-gut*, the words of the head shaman were relayed to me through the middle *manshin*. I was not yet in a position to dare speak directly with the great head *manshin*. I could sense the extremely stern laws of the spirit world.

"What will you become in the future?" my grandmother asked, but that was something I could not know. I was about to respond that I didn't yet know when a bizarre answer came out of my mouth instead.

---

60. 물베바치기, a ritual dedicated to *Yongwang* (God of Water, also translated as Dragon King), using water to foresee the success of the *mudang's* career.

61. 일월다리, represents the connecting bridge the Celestial God descends on.

"I will attain a higher rank than the venerable and divine priestly official of *nara-manshin*.[62]"

A thunderous outburst of rage erupted from my grandmother as soon as I uttered those words.

"You insolent wench! What do you mean by attaining a higher rank? Do you dare belittle the great and divine priestly official *man-shins* by spewing such contemptuous nonsense? Strike her legs!"

The younger *manshins* in the courtyard struck my calves with all their might. Each time the oak tree branches hit my calves, I felt like my flesh was sliced by sharp ice. My grandmother asked once again what I wanted to become.

My response this time was very modest. "I want to become a great *mudang*."

"Now, receive the gods descending on you and serve them."

I stood and began to dance. My body movements became more impassioned as I danced, and my hair stood on end. At that moment, I felt the presence of the gods enter my body. I offered up the names of each god one by one, and the procession seemed endless. Beginning with *Ilweolseongshin, Bukdu-DaeSeong,*[63] *Sanshin, Cheonhadaesin Janggun,*[64] *Im Gyeong-eop*[65] *Janggun, Shinjang-nim,*[66] and others. Despite feeling weary and exhausted, once I danced channeling these gods, my body felt as light as if I were flying.

---

62. 나라만신, a nation's shaman or an imperial shaman. During the Joseon Dynasty, the *mudang* responsible for performing rituals commissioned by the state and the royal court.

63. 북두대성, the great north star, also *Chilseong-shin* (칠성신).

64. 천하대신 장군, the Divine Warrior General God.

65. 임경업 (1594–1646 CE), a famous warrior general during the Joseon Dynasty, tied to the Shamanic rituals of fishing villages.

66. 신장, a guardian deity known for defeating and chasing out evil and lowly spirits.

Finally, my grandmother spoke to me directly. "Becoming a *manshin* is to endure much unbearable pain that no ordinary person can withstand."

Only then did I look at the people surrounding me. My mother had long been crying in the corner. The faces of my clueless younger siblings looked at me with fear, stained by tears and runny noses. Perhaps I no longer felt like their older sister. Even if I became a *mudang*, I could not wash away the poverty and sorrow of my poor, wretched family. If anything, we had sunk even lower now, having two *mudangs* in our home. Even if it was an undesired outcome, I had no choice but to live under the shadow of Divine Spirit. Since *mudangs* at that time belonged to the lowest social class, I would have to carry wounds in my heart. Alas, that was my fate now.

I wept because I felt sorry for my mother, who had been lonely for a long time after losing her husband much too young. I wailed bitterly for my siblings, who had never eaten a full meal and worked in the fields with faces bloated with hunger.

During the passage of *Jaeseok-gut*,[67] my grandmother gave me a long *gongsu*[68] with great care. Her calloused hands tightly held onto mine.

"When I saw you, so full of spirit energy, I found it as unbearable as a fire charring the inside of my heart. Watching you wandering the fields without a single friend, suffering from so much sickness, and getting scrawny as a skewer broke my heart. I wondered why my granddaughter Neomse couldn't just have fun and enjoy life like other children. When I saw signs that you might

---

67. 제석굿, a passage of the *gut* dedicated in honor of *Jeseok-shin*, the deity of divination and healing.

68. 공수, the divine words and spirit messages which a *mudang* replays and channels during rituals.

be following in my footsteps, I would curse you and chase you away from me, but you would cling to me even more fiercely. I cried and begged the gods not to make my Neomse a *mudang*. I prayed every night, promising this old-timer would gladly suffer any pain or harsh punishment if only Neomse could be spared. It breaks my heart to think that this poor little thing, who never received proper food, warmth, or love, must now become a *mudang* and suffer countless scars in this harsh and bitter world."

With tears streaming down her face, my grandmother squeezed my hand even tighter. Her voice choked up, and her *gongsu* became increasingly hoarse.

"But this humble old woman is too human and inadequate to discern the will of Great Spirit. The more I tried to stop you, the closer Spirit called you. Now, Spirit commands me to make you, a beautiful flower, my new disciple, to continue my path. With such great and noble gods bestowed upon you, be as high and mighty as the sky and the sea. Even if you fall and fall again, rely on your gods and Divine Spirit to rise anew. As your grandmother, it breaks my heart that I have never been able to treat you with kindness in the human world."

Before she could finish the *gongsu*, my grandmother leaned against me as if collapsing and shed tears endlessly. At that moment, my great and intimidating grandmother felt so small, her body so light that I burst into tears myself.

Ah, Great Spirit, thank you for making me a mudang *and allowing me to become my grandmother's spirit daughter.*

Unknowingly, I found myself giving profound thanks to the presence of Divine Spirit within me.

Ah, this is what it's all about. It's so wonderful to see people loving one another, letting go of old grievances, and embracing each other. It is heartening to hold hands, comfort one another, and sincerely fathom each other's hearts.

On that day, I released all the sorrow and *han*[69] buried in my heart for the past seventeen years.

From now on, I will not hold grudges against anything or anyone. Instead, I will hold and embrace everything. Great Spirit, please watch over me and guide me for a long, long time.

The sorrow, hunger, pain, and resentment stemming from an unwelcoming childhood were shed away through my burning tears. Family members and people from the neighborhood clung to each other and wept together.

When it was time for the *jakdu* passage, I confidently mounted the knives and offered *gongsu* to everyone. It felt like those who had once rejected and despised me—my maternal grandmother, neighbors, and friends—had become like one family. I offered *gongsu* clumsily yet wholeheartedly, not leaving out a single person. I also gave it to myself, saying, "I will face many deaths as I embark on the divine path."

Then I made a vow repeatedly in my heart: *I will undoubtedly become a great* mudang. *A powerful and fearless one!*

---

69. 한, a uniquely Korean term of burden in body and soul, an internalized feeling that blends deep sorrow, resentment, grief, regret, and anger, believed to have originated due to Korea's long history of invasion, oppression, and suffering.

TEN

A Rigorous *Mudang* Training

Receiving a *Naerim-gut* does not automatically make one a *mudang*. To become a proper *mudang*, one must have a good spirit mother and diligently attend *gut* rituals for at least four years to learn various procedures. One is not sat down and spoon-fed knowledge. Learning involves observing and absorbing what one's spirit mother and elder *manshins* do through one's eyes, ears, and other senses. If one fails to properly learn the twelve passages of the *gut*, despite receiving the gods and deities to serve, one cannot lead a proper *mudang* life and may be relegated to a mere fortuneteller or remain an incompetent novice *mudang*.

I also underwent intense *mudang* training. Because my spirit mother, my maternal grandmother, was in poor health, I learned the *gut* rituals by following other *manshins*. The teachings of these strict elder *manshins* were even more demanding in some ways than what I endured with my past mother-in-law.

The very first thing I learned was how to fold *mubok*, the

ceremonial robes. I must have repeated the task of folding *gwaeja*, the long sleeveless robes, countless times. Shamanic attire must be folded upright, a reminder to always stand tall and grow. When folding clothes, one must maintain a proper posture and do so skillfully. I was scolded for lack of respect for the gods when I laid the apparel on the floor or failed to fold it neatly. After each passage of the *gut*, I carefully folded any *mubok* that were thrown haphazardly aside. I also learned how to shake the Shamanic rattle. I joyfully mastered the art of holding the rattles, shaking them gracefully, and playing the *jegeum* to the beat.

The most crucial element in a *gut* is the *muga*, the Shamanic songs. Each passage of the *gut* has its own *muga*, characterized by diverse rhythms and extensive lyrics. It is not an easy task to learn them all. This could not be memorized from a book or written down on paper; it was learned purely through one's attentive ears and lips. Not lacking in intellectual capacity, I could remember the lengthy Shamanic songs without difficulty. Whenever I listened to a Shamanic song, I intensely focused my mind and made sure not to miss a single word.

A new *manshin's* place was always next to the *jing*, the gong. Even while learning the songs, the novice shaman had to stand beside the senior *manshin* and oversee the gong. I once stood next to the *janggu* drum and was harshly reprimanded. The metallic sound of the gong was thought to help the new shaman open their spirit ears, and if I ever moved closer to the *janggu* drum, the drumstick would be hurled at my feet.

One day, my teacher had a new disciple. When the new student entered, the teacher suddenly gestured at me to step aside. Without thinking, I moved aside. At that moment, out of nowhere, the stick struck me directly on my ankle bone. I let out a brief yelp and slumped down in dizzying pain. Everyone's eyes immediately fixed on me. The pain from being struck was one thing, but having everyone's attention on me was worse. I retreated backward like a crayfish trying to escape, but my eyes locked with those of the elder *manshin* teacher. She widened her eyes even more and glared at me as if she wanted to eat me alive. With no choice, I returned to my original place, pretending to adjust my skirt and socks. I cleared my throat and tried to sing along, but tears welled up, and my throat tightened, making it difficult. Despite my efforts, a teardrop plopped onto the gong. After that incident, I never stood near the *janggu* again, so it was indeed an effective lesson learned.

* * *

Wherever there was a *gut*, I attended, even if it was dozens of *li* away, to help and learn. It wasn't just about learning the different passages; I massaged the legs of the elderly *manshins* for hours after the ritual and prepared snacks at the appropriate time. Taking care of the *manshins'* straw shoes was a basic duty, and I also had to ensure that their bedding and wash water was ready. All these tasks were to be carried out with absolute cleanliness. When a great *manshin* showed signs of heading to the outhouse, I knew to quickly follow without needing instruction. A novice shaman stood by the outhouse and vigorously rubbed straws together to soften them before handing them over for wiping. It was also said that novice shamans should not eat much since it hinders their ability to jump and dance. It was believed that eating sparingly kept one's spirit clear, enhanced the ability to hear the gods, and ensured the success of the *gut*.

After a few months, I was entrusted with tending to the knives and attire for the various *gut* passages. If I happened to bring the wrong garments or tools, the senior shaman would knock them out of my hands and give me a stern look. Even as I served them on my hands and knees, the elder *manshins* never offered a lesson or teaching. If, after much hesitation, I mustered the courage to ask a question, I was met with a chilly reprimand. I was meant to reach understanding by observing, listening, and figuring things out on my own. It was believed that only then would I learn to approach divine work with utmost care and dedication—and I suppose there is sound reasoning behind this approach.

When a novice becomes adept at serving and learning the *gut*, she is then given the responsibility of leading one or two of the *gut* passages. One day, my spirit mother entrusted me with performing *Seongju-gut*, a ritual for a household's guardian deity. I performed the ritual and danced as best as I had learned. However, it seemed as if she was not at all satisfied.

"Have you left your ears behind? Are your eyes scaled over? What a mess. Is that a *gut* or just waddling around?"

The great *manshin* barreled towards me and swiftly stripped me of the ritual robe, snatching the tools from my hand and performing the *gut* herself. My face burned as if engulfed in flames, and I felt utterly lost as to where to even stand. But I had to quickly regain composure. Despite the overwhelming shame and humiliation that burned fiercely behind my eyes, I kept the tears away.

Still, thanks to rigorous training and effort, I was able to perform a *gut* on my own after less than a year of shadowing the other *manshins*. After serving and learning from the great *manshins* and leading one or two passages of *guts*, I gradually gained recognition from people for my own ritual practices. Word spread, and people sought me to perform their *guts*. Even though I performed these *guts* on my own, I continued to shadow the great *manshins* whenever possible to fill my knowledge gaps.

Those chosen by Divine Spirit should accept and serve Spirit with a joyful heart. For one destined to become a great *mudang*, the initiation ritual and their interaction with the gods happen with awesome power and might. When powerful ancestral spirits from higher realms descend, or one is called from the lineage of many ancestors, she can become an even greater shaman. However, even the spirits that are not powerful in their might, once they descend, must be received and served well. When one serves the spirits with respect and devotion regardless of their powers, all spirits will offer care, giving protection and blessings.

There are cases when one's destiny changes upon the descent of the spirits. When one receives a benevolent spirit, one's personality can improve. But to become a better *manshin*, a great *manshin*, one must constantly strive on their own. Rushing along this path can lead to ruin. By maintaining a firmness of will and approaching the calling with a joyful heart, one can live as a good *manshin* who helps many people.

ELEVEN

I Will Walk the Path of a Great Shaman

In less than a year since undergoing the *Naerim-gut* initiation, I was called to perform *guts* in many different places. Even though I was still a newly emerged novice *manshin*, I spent a very busy year performing a variety of *guts*, including the illness *gut* and the blessing *gut*. As a result, I lost my voice by the time the next Lunar year arrived. Many customers sought divination for the New Year, and I couldn't do anything as a shaman. I felt terrible for turning away the visitors who had traveled from afar.

What can be done? I wondered to myself. *Maybe I did something wrong?*

"What did you dream on the last day of the month?" my grandmother asked me as she noticed my worry.

I shared my dream with her. In my dream, I was riding a red horse, and there was a swing swaying back and forth in front of me, so I quickly climbed onto it. Then the swing ascended to a mountain, where I saw a twisted pine tree before me. I jumped off the swing and climbed onto the tree.

"Did the swing go forward or backward?" my grandmother asked.

"It only went forward."

"It's a good dream, foretelling immense blessings," she assured me. "Wait and see."

It must have been around the eighth day of the first Lunar month when I received my first call to perform a *Daedong-gut*, a ritual reserved for the greatest experienced and knowledgeable *manshins* due to its large scale. The *gut* was to take place in an island village on Yongho Island. The village had a chief *baksu*,[70] but for the past few years, they hadn't seen any good results with him, so the villagers decided to invite a new, promising novice *manshin* for this *Daedong-gut*. I felt very excited about the opportunity, but anxiety soon took over. *Daedong-gut*, held continuously for five straight days, was difficult even for experienced *manshins*. Moreover, I had lost my voice, and I wasn't sure if I would be able to perform even one passage of the long *gut*.

"You've come such a long way, but what can we do? Look, my daughter has lost her voice..." My mother apologized to the island villagers with a remorseful expression.

But upon hearing this, my grandmother burst out angrily, "Ah, what kind of *mudang* refuses to perform a *Daedong-gut* because she lost her voice? What about spirits? Bring me the *janggu* drum from over there."

My grandmother played the *janggu*, suggesting we should attempt a household *gut* as a test. I had no choice but to follow her instructions. I held the bells and fan and began to dance.

"Hurrah, *Manse!*"

---

70. 박수, a male *mudang*.

As I began, something amazing happened. *Was that a clear sound emanating from my throat?*

"What nonsense about losing your voice!"

The people from Yongho Island felt relieved and happily returned home. I spent several days eagerly anticipating the *gut*. Finally, it was the day before the *gut*. When we reached the pier, we found the villagers murmuring worriedly. A ship was scheduled to arrive at Yongho Island for the ritual, but suddenly, a storm arose, and it couldn't dock at the pier, so it turned back. People were filled with anxiety and dread that the carefully arranged and anticipated *gut* might not take place. However, strangely, my heart was at ease.

"The gods will assist us."

As night fell, the storm unexpectedly subsided. We gathered branches and twigs and set them ablaze—a signal to send the ship. From the opposite shore, a bonfire was ignited in response.

"All is well now!" People clapped their hands and shouted with joy.

Yongho Island consisted of a large fishing village of around 400 households. It had a reputation for generosity and strong unity among the villagers, making it a thriving community. As I contemplated that the welfare and hopes of the entire village rested on the performance of this *gut*—on my shoulders—I felt an even greater sense of responsibility. I resolved to devote myself entirely to performing the *gut*. I had faith that if I exerted my utmost effort, the spirits would undoubtedly provide their assistance.

The next day, I purified my body and climbed the mountain with the village elders at dawn to prepare for the *gut*. Upon descending, I changed into clean undergarments and donned a flowered *gat*[71] and new straw shoes, preparing for the ceremony.

---

71. 갓, a traditional Korean hat made of bamboo and horsehair.

As the sun rose, casting a scarlet hue, we set off for the house where the ritual would be held. While passing through the outskirts of the village towards the mountain, I couldn't help but doubt my eyes. I was awed and thrilled, and my heart felt like it was leaping out of my chest. It appeared that all the people of Yongho Island had gathered on the beach. Dressed in dazzling white attire, they lined up along the blue shoreline. Colorful flowers adorned the branches of nearby willow trees, swaying and fluttering in the wind.

People took a few steps back and cleared the way as we walked by. Everyone held their breath and waited for us to pass. No one obstructed our path. My nose felt sore and tingly, and tears were welling up in my eyes.

I never imagined I would experience a day like this. A day where I can stand confidently and receive such an extraordinary reception from the people...

As I recalled the challenging days of the past, waves of both sadness and deep emotion engulfed me. I held back hot tears— tears I couldn't afford to show in front of such a large audience. With a resolute spirit, I lowered my gaze and continued walking.

"Oh dear, she's just a child, a baby!"

"Do you think such a fragile body can endure five days of ritual? Tsk tsk..."

"Her steps are so graceful."

As I passed, I heard murmurs of concern coming from all around. But the *gut* went very well. The sacred wooden pole, shaken vigorously when possessed by *Seonang-shin*,[72] entered the basin of pure water.

"Oh my, our village will receive abundant blessings from this *Daedong-gut!*"

The people expressed their joy. I, too, felt a sense of happiness

---

72. 서낭신, the deity who protects the land and surrounding village.

because I had a premonition that the *gut* would be successful. The divine energy that was channeled remained powerful throughout the five days. When it was time for *segyeongdoli*,[73] I declined the food prepared in each home as I traveled around the entire village. I didn't even notice my hunger.

As I traversed the village, following the swaying of the sacred pole, I was led into government offices and the police station. Having experienced harassment from law enforcement in the past, I was scared, but these officers here were different. Here, they respectfully bowed to me, handed me a yellow offering envelope, and prayed earnestly. I was encouraged to see support from those whom I had always assumed rejected *guts* and *man-shins*. My heart stayed full each of the five days, and I successfully completed the *gut*.

"You perform the *gut* so well!"

"You're as graceful as a dancing butterfly."

I gave *gongsu* earnestly to the villagers. Not wanting to miss a single word, people leaned in to listen, their eyes shining. Hot tears streamed from my eyes as I realized each divine word I spoke contained the blessings and aspirations of the people. I was profoundly grateful and expressed my thanks to Divine Spirit for helping me despite my shortcomings.

From now on, I will walk the path of a great shaman.

When my mother arrived two days later, people showered her with exuberant praise. My mother quietly wiped away her tears with the hem of her skirt.

On the sixth day following the five consecutive days of the *gut*, I loaded a cart full of rice, rice cakes, and beef and made my way to the dock. The cart was adorned with various colorful flowers,

---

73. 세경돌이, a ritual in which a *mudang* walks a village guided by the sacred pole, offering blessings and words to the people.

making me feel like a *seonnyo*[74] in a field of blossoms. My ritual crew and I returned home triumphantly sounding the boat horn.

"*Aigoo,* what a glorious return!"

My grandmother rushed out barefoot to greet me. I flew to the ground and bowed deeply, weeping on my knees for a long time. My grandmother and mother also wept alongside me. All at once, memories resurfaced of being bullied and ridiculed, having to hide the wounds in our hearts simply because we belonged to a Shamanic family. After such an extended period of hunger and loneliness, here was the day when the pitiable Neomse, who seemed unlikely to lead a life of meaning, returned home with pride after bringing joy to Divine Spirit and earning the honor and respect of countless people.

---

74. 선녀, a heavenly maiden.

Longing for My Hometown

Even now, when I close my eyes, the mountains and sea of my hometown are vividly painted in my mind. On days when life as a *mudang* is exhausting, I long for my hometown even more. Even the memories of hunger and hardship in my youth occasionally make my heart ache with longing. The mountains and fields of my childhood always seem to embrace me warmly, as if they will be there forever to hold me.

As a child, what I eagerly awaited the most was the holidays. In the last Lunar month of the year, my maternal grandfather would gift me a beautiful pair of straw shoes. Wearing these straw shoes, woven with colorful fabric, there was nothing to envy—not even silk flower shoes. My maternal grandmother would sew me a gorgeous *hanbok* with a deep blue skirt and a yellow *jeogori* jacket with purple trim. Then she styled my hair, skillfully folding the silken *daenggi*[75] ribbon into my long braid.

---

75. 댕기, a traditional hair ribbon.

As *Seollal*[76] approached, I was so happy and excited that I couldn't sleep. On the holidays, I could eat foods that I had not been able to enjoy before. *Ojangchatteok* was prepared—an *injeolmi* rice cake filled with sweetened white beans and a sweet rice drink. Bean sprouts were grown in earthenware pots in advance of the holiday feast. Soybean curd, *doenjang*, pumpkin, and several yellow corvina fish were placed on the ceremonial table, ensuring a proper celebration of the Lunar New Year.

I barely ate breakfast, dressed in my new clothes, met with friends, and visited neighborhood homes, bowing to offer New Year's greetings. In some homes, I received a sweet rice drink, while in others, I was treated to *injeolmi* rice cakes dipped in sweet syrup, melting smoothly in my mouth. It was a delicacy among delicacies, a special treat. We enjoyed delicious food and shared various stories with one another. But our main interest was to observe what clothes each person wore.

During the first Lunar month, we practiced many fun customs associated with bringing good fortune. On the first grand full moon, people hung wide, round weaved trays in front of their front gates to be filled with blessings. It was believed to bring bad luck if the evil goddess descended from the sky to try on your shoes, so we got busy hiding them. After hiding our shoes, we stayed up all night, talking. It was said that if you fell asleep on the full moon of the first Lunar month, your eyebrows and hair would turn white. Occasionally, when a child fell asleep, we would playfully sprinkle flour on their heads and visit another home.

There were various ways to determine one's fortune for the year. We would fill a plate with oil and make wicks with cotton wool, lighting as many wicks as the number of family members and naming each one for a member of the household. Then we

---

76. 설날, Lunar New Year

observed which flame was the biggest and brightest. If a flame was dim, it was said to be a sign of illness, but if a flame was large and burnt steadily without smoking, it was considered a sign of good health and good things to come.

Family members also filled rice bowls with water and placed them on earthenware pots outside. It was thought that one could predict one's fortune by observing the shape of the water freezing in the bowl. If the water had risen like a column, or if the center of the ice grew more than the rest, it was believed to be an auspicious sign of blessings. If the water froze only in the center, it was a sign of abundant farming and other happy things. If the middle sank, however, it signified impending illness, and if the center became concave or tilted to one side, it was understood as a sign of ill health and considered unlucky.

Sorghum stalks were also used to predict the farming prospects for the year. After cutting the stalks, a bean was inserted into the middle of the cut section, and each limb was numbered from the first month to the twelfth month. Early in the evening of the following day, the stalks were placed in a well.

"*Yongwang-nim*, God of Water, we want to see the forecasted drought and flooding for the year. Please provide a detailed answer."

Then, on the morning of the full moon, the sorghum stalks left in the well were retrieved for interpretation. Some of the beans placed in the stalks were plump and swollen, while others were less so. It was said that well-swollen beans indicated heavy rainfall during the rainy season.

Nowadays, such practices are often dismissed and ridiculed as superstition, but back then, generations deeply revered the customs passed down by our ancestors. Despite our poverty, there was a spirit of sharing even the most minor things among family members and neighbors and a deep respect for elders and their traditions.

For example, when my father worked as a field hand, he sometimes returned home with a yellow corvina wrapped in paper. He would serve the body of the fish to my grandfather, then, with a sigh, allow us children to eat the fish head. As I grew older, I realized that my father saved the fish offered as his daily meal in exchange for his labor, bringing it home for his family instead. Meanwhile, he only ate a tiny fluff of millet rice for his meal, although he worked all day long. I remember the day he told me, with a long sigh, about nearly choking to death on bloated millet that he swallowed too hurriedly.

In those days, whenever it was time for planting or harvesting rice fields, people from the village would help one another without hesitation. For the helpers, lunch was bean sprout rice and soybean paste soup with wild vegetable leaves, served communally from a large bowl. Each person also received a yellow corvina fish as a side dish. Not a single person would eat the entire fish. Some would only eat the head or tail, while others would cut the fish in half, consuming half and saving the other half to take home. No one regarded this practice as pathetic or ridiculous.

The household where the fields were being worked would rise early in the morning to cook plenty of rice mixed with red beans before packing it into the large wooden bowl. The soybean paste soup with vegetable stems was stored in jugs, and two women carried the food to the fields on top of their heads. This act was known as "bringing the *bapgori*." [77] If there were many laborers, they carried the food bowls in large baskets in the morning and placed them by the side of the rice fields in advance. After the laborers finished their lunches, the *bapgori* was gathered and brought back home.

Next, the family would invite all the elderly women and

---

77. 밥고리, an old dialect referring to a lunch box.

men of the village to gather over what food was left. Of course, the people already knew when the *bapgori* had been taken out and returned, as they had sent children to find out. But it was only when they heard the children going from house to house, calling, "Please come have lunch at so-and-so's house," that they would straighten their bent backs and walk along. The homes with housebound elders or sick persons were not forgotten either. The prepared food was evenly distributed in the large wooden bowl and sent to each home. In homes where an elder had passed away and a mourning altar had been set up, carefully arranged food and dishes were offered as a mourning meal as well.

Taking care of a mourning altar was not limited to the houses on *bapgori* duty. Even during marriage rituals, noodles, rice cakes, and alcohol were first sent to homes with mourning altars. The families who received these offerings would gratefully accept the food, offering it to the ancestral altar by announcing, "So-and-so's home is celebrating, and they brought food. Please partake in the meal." There was no distinction between the living and the dead when it came to honoring the elders.

I, too, ran around the village, gathering elderly people and taking them to meal gatherings. These elderly, so hungry their stomachs growled loudly, relished the fattened and deliciously grilled corvina fish, including the skin. Observing such scenes, we naturally learned to honor our elders. Reflecting on it now, it was truly a beautiful virtue to cultivate, the village elderly acting as a living education and example for future generations.

It is much harder to find such virtues these days. My heart aches when I see news about elderly people discovered dead and alone, often after several days of neglect or more. Why isn't it still common to consider that we each owe our very existence to these elderly instead of treating them as useless waste? It's vital for us to realize that our actions towards our elders are precisely what our children observe and learn from. Whenever I witness these harsh realities of the world, I reminisce about my childhood hometown. Even though those times were lean and challenging, I desperately miss all the people I knew who had generous and pure hearts.

A photo taken with a client's family when Kim Keum-Hwa was 25 years old. She was the sixth *mudang* to be called to perform an illness ritual for the young man who was suffering from a mental illness. His symptoms miraculously disappeared after her ritual.

A photo taken with two friends when Kim Keum-Hwa was around 24. It was difficult to make many friends in her life as a *manshin*, but there were always a few who deeply cared about her.

A photo during a *Cheolmuri-gut* circa 1978. This *gut* was done by the villagers to welcome the new season, and its tradition dates back to the time of Dangun.

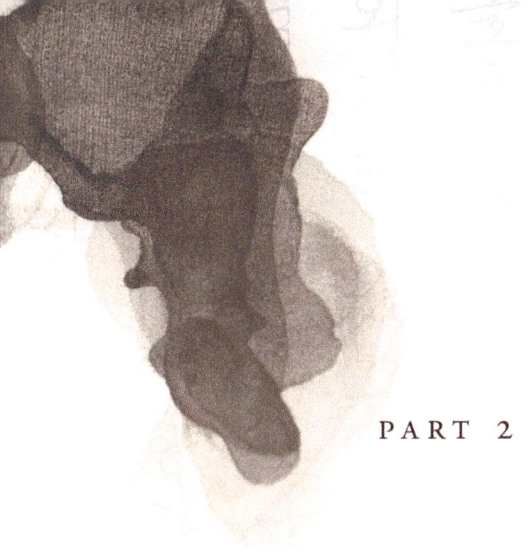

PART 2

"Why Did You Become a Shaman?"

A *mudang* is one who embraces and consoles the *han*
and tears of all. Because I have been wounded and have
shed many tears over human affairs, I am able to better
understand and comfort those who come to me.

by Kim Keum-Hwa

THIRTEEN

A Gut Performed at Gunpoint

On the day I received the *Naerim-gut*, I gave myself a *gongsu*—an oracle—that said, 'I will go through many deaths on this path set forth by Divine Spirit.' How did I see so clearly this path would be anything but smooth? On several occasions, I've had to risk my very life to perform a *gut* and uphold the role of *mudang*.

One such incident occurred when it seemed the entire world was in chaos after the January Fourth Retreat (the Third Battle of Seoul[78]). There was a South Korean security unit called *Cheongbang* in the village whose behavior was so violent that people walked around with fearful and downcast faces. You couldn't even think about performing a *gut* or divination. Yet people with anxiety from the war secretly sought me out to inquire about their future and to check if their family members were still alive.

---

78. On January 4, 1951, the Chinese military entered the Korean War, pushing UN soldiers to retreat south of Seoul.

Around the last month of the Lunar year, with a sharp wind fiercely blowing, a middle-aged woman came to visit me in the middle of the night.

"Is the *manshin* in?"

She was a regular client who used to ask for the blessing *gut* every three years. Her son-in-law was a chief administrator in the Navy's CID,[79] but he had a lung disease and was close to dying. The military medical officers had diagnosed him with advanced stage 3 pulmonary tuberculosis, declaring it fatal. She wanted me to perform a *gut* to ensure his peaceful passage so he may die without remorse.

The woman, with a pale and virtuous-looking face, was always generous and loving in her heart, so she tended to see good outcomes from performing *guts*. Since she had long cherished and loved her son-in-law as if he were her own son, she wanted to call for a *gut* to at least provide solace during his sudden departure from this life.

I performed a quick *songobi*[80] divination using my hand. Contrary to the woman's expectations, my senses indicated that he might recover after a *gut*. However, since this was a matter of life and death, I hesitated to say anything and sent her away.

A few days later, on the twenty-ninth day of the last month of the Lunar year, I purified my body and headed to the patient's house. While carrying everything needed for the ritual on my shoulders without anyone to assist me, I met a local man on the road.

"How can anyone request a *gut* these days in such a harsh and dangerous world? Who knows what that might bring upon you?" he chastised.

---

79. Criminal Investigation Division.

80. 손고비, a quick divination a *mudang* performed using her hand without receiving any payment, often as an assessment tool.

The man, a military medical officer, looked at me with concern because he knew the patient's illness was incurable. I was also deeply worried. Persecution at the hands of CID was unbearable. How many accusations and hateful glares did I receive from them for being a *mudang*? How often was I accused of needlessly disturbing and unsettling people's minds? They even accused me of engaging in espionage, on several occasions going as far as threatening to shoot me. If I were caught performing a *gut*, it would be a convenient excuse for them to finally kill me. Suddenly, it felt like a gun was pointed at my neck, sending chills down my spine. However, allowing worries to consume me on my way to perform a *gut* would only lead to negativity. I allowed myself to entrust everything to Great Spirit, believing Spirit would surely help, as always. After gathering up courage in my heart, I hurried on my way.

The patient, whose surname was Park, was thirty-three years old. Park, once a chief administrator in the CID, was known for his decent and kind behavior, earning him a good reputation among the villagers.

In a single glance, it was evident that the patient's condition was beyond recovery. He coughed up thick blood into a chamber pot. Due to his inability to eat, he had become thin as a scarecrow, and his face was so pale it took on a bluish tint. Despite the fraught circumstances, several people who had already heard I was coming arrived to help with the *gut*. When I arrived, a man and a woman, who appeared to be military medical officers, were caring for the patient.

"Who performs a *gut* for a pulmonary disease?"

A mean-looking female medical officer stared at me with contempt and left. As I set up the *gut*, the patient's condition worsened, and he went in and out of consciousness. But whenever he was conscious, he looked up at me with a faint smile.

The *gut* commenced in the evening and continued throughout the entire night. At first, I was tense, perhaps due to my own anxiety and desperation, and the *gut* didn't begin well. However, as time passed, I forgot about my human existence and immersed myself in the world of Spirit, with only the patient's welfare in my heart.

KungTukTuk, KungTukTuk, ChangGang ChangGang...

Encouraged by the sound of the *janggu* and *jegeum*, I danced so fast that my feet were almost invisible. With each passage of the *gut*, I was pulled more powerfully into the world of spirits.

At the end of the *Jeseok-gut*,[81] I called the patient to the center of the *gut* stage and told him to dance. With a respectful expression and leaning on the support of his mother-in-law and wife, the patient managed to reach the front of the *janggu*, only to collapse on the floor. He could only mimic the dance faintly while seated. I draped an ancestral cloth over Park's shoulders and began dancing. Then he asked to be helped up. With the assistance of his family, Park stood up and danced with his arms raised, just as he had done while seated. He danced and spun around several times, despite the fact that just moments ago, even sitting up had been exhausting for him.

Ah, I can see hope.

Yet it wasn't easy. Every time Park stood upright, his body faltered. When he tried to spin around, his feet gave out. Eventually, he just lay flat on the ground. No matter how I looked at it, his condition seemed hopeless. I thought to myself that when the time came for the *gongsu*, I would have to say, "There's no resolving this. You will die soon." I was not confident in bearing

---

81. 제석굿, a healing ritual.

the responsibility or handling the aftermath of telling a dying person they would live. Moreover, members of the patient's CID unit watched me with intensely fierce gazes. I glimpsed the glint of gun barrels on their shoulders.

As I danced on the *jakdu* knives and offered *gongsu*, I intended to say, "*Hey, hey,* this thirty-three-year-old man of the Park family won't live past the day after tomorrow."

But instead, I blurted out, "You will start healing the day after tomorrow." When I wanted to say, "You must prepare to depart this world..." what unexpectedly popped out of my mouth was, "Don't you worry, I'll help you walk on solid ground as you used to."

Sweating profusely like rain, I stepped off the *jakdu*. Immediately, my chest felt the coldness of a gun barrel pointed at me.

"Death by firing squad!" the patient's superior, the chief of the CID, shouted.

He glared at me with a stern expression, as if he had reached his limit. The patient's mother-in-law panicked and tried to restrain him. But he did not back down easily.

"Do you know how many members of my unit I have lost when they have gone out to the fields in search of a single grain of rice? Yet here you are, wasting precious rice by making rice cakes and talking nonsense. Are you providing medicine or giving out injections? Can you cure someone by making rice cakes and dancing your stupid dance? Get up and leave so you can face the firing squad!"

He forcefully struck me on the back with the barrel of his gun. I crumpled forward from the impact. The frightened mother-in-law and wife pleaded with the chief. They explained they were the ones who requested the *gut* and that it had been hard to arrange. They begged him to kindly understand just this once. Upon hearing their plea, the man glanced at the patient and then turned to ask me a question.

"Our administrative chief, when did you say he would get better?"

"He will get better the day after tomorrow." My voice trembled as I spoke.

"You have until then. If Park doesn't recover by the day after tomorrow, you will surely be shot to death."

He pointed the gun at my throat once more and then left with the other soldiers. After finishing the *gut*, I hurriedly returned home. When I lay down for the evening, sleep eluded me.

Will he really recover by the day after tomorrow? I wondered. *When he couldn't even stand?*

Overcome with anxiety, I went out to the backyard, fetched water from the well, and bathed myself. The water was freezing cold and crackled with chunks of ice. After finishing my bath, I filled a large earthenware pot with water and prostrated myself before it. I repeatedly rubbed my freezing, reddened hands in prayer.

"Oh, Divine Spirit, I am still so young. I have only just begun to serve you properly, and here I am facing death. Spirit, I offered up a *gut* with all my heart. Please help me."

I could not sleep for two straight nights.

The promised day dawned. I thought about running away, but there was no place to hide during those turbulent times, and I was also extremely curious about the patient's condition.

Day and night, I have prayed and served others, yet why is my own situation so pathetic? I wondered to myself, hesitating at my front gate.

Unable to step out, I stood on the threshold, gazing towards the village where I had performed the *gut*. After remaining there for a while, the face of Park's mother-in-law suddenly appeared from around the corner near the straw mill. I was surprised. My heart raced, and I wondered if something had gone wrong. But when I looked closely, I could see she was smiling radiantly. Only then did I exhale a sigh of relief. The woman rushed towards me and tightly grasped both of my hands.

"He's no longer vomiting blood! He's eating porridge, and vitality has returned to him. Thank you so much!"

Tears welled up in the woman's eyes. She had rushed over to deliver the good news of her son-in-law's improving condition. Divine Spirit had helped. Without looking back, I ran towards my shrine. Falling on my knees before it, I wept tears of gratitude.

"Thank you so much for accepting my humble prayers. I am truly thankful."

* * *

Many years later, long after I had sought refuge in southern Korea during the war, I saw Mr. Park, the patient, again.

Around 1960, following the April 19th Revolution and the resignation of President Syngman Rhee, I was summoned to perform a small *Jaesu-gut*[82] just before the local elections on a small island called Yongyu. Mr. Park was working as a clerk at Yongyu Island's township office, handling military registration-related matters. The islanders, known for their strong regionalism and bias against officials, looked down upon and disliked Mr. Park, a refugee and an outsider. The only reason Mr. Park managed to keep his position as secretary was due to Chief Cho's assistance. However, it was time for a new election for the township's chief position.

Anxious and worried, given that his entire family's livelihood

---

82. 재수굿, a *gut* performed for the flourishing and prosperity of a household.

depended on him retaining his position, Mr. Park requested a *Jaesu-gut*: a *gut* to carry the family's fervent wishes that Chief Cho would be reelected, ensuring Mr. Park's secretary position. I performed the *gut* wholeheartedly and returned home. After about two weeks, I had a strange dream in which Yongyu Island's township election took place on a sandy shore of the riverbank. Someone called for Chief Cho to be elected, so people in line sealed their stamps next to Cho's name. But after watching from the sidelines, I said, "Isn't Mr. Park better than Chief Cho? Let's make Park the new chief." Upon hearing my words, people pressed their seals firmly next to Park's name.

I thought it was a peculiar and nonsensical dream. Mr. Park would be considered fortunate just to keep his current position, so the idea of him becoming the chief seemed far-fetched. But after a month or two, someone from my hometown stopped by to deliver news about Yongyu Island. I was confident that Cho had been reelected as the township chief and asked about it. To my surprise, I received the strange news that Mr. Park had become the new chief. Even the person delivering the information found it unexpected, tilting his head in confusion. Surprised and delighted, I returned to Yongyu Island to congratulate Mr. Park.

"I don't know how to express my thanks to you for opening up good pathways for me several times." Mr. Park smiled at me broadly with his gentle face and expressed his gratitude.

Some people reject and ostracize shamans and our *gut* rituals as useless superstitions. However, how can one dismiss as meaningless superstition the sacred energy that has saved the life of a young person on the brink of death and continued to watch over and guide his destiny for a long time?

FOURTEEN

A Sincere Heart
Moves Heavens

When I first fled to the South during the war, I lived in a small shack consisting of a single room and a kitchen behind the police station in Manseok-dong, Incheon. One day, an elderly woman entered the home, looking for me.

"Is the new *manshin* in?"

The person who stepped through the squat doorway, so small that even a tiny person had to hunch, was none other than the neighbor who had lived next door in my hometown in the North.

"I was wondering what I would do if you weren't home, but here you are," she said.

"*Ajumai*, how did you know to come here? Please come in and have a seat."

Overwhelmed with joy at meeting someone from my hometown, I took her hand and guided her to sit beside me. Before she even sat down, the woman began speaking about the purpose of her visit.

"*Ya*, I rushed over here in a hurry. Come do a *songobi* right now!" She pestered me to start a quick-hand divination.

"Who do you want me to perform a *songobi* for?"

"It's the Kim kid from our Chong family. He's been sick for three days now. His eyes are bloodshot like a pig's head on an altar, and he's shaking uncontrollably, muttering and spewing nonsense. What must we do?" She mentioned that the doctor had already visited twice with no improvement.

"Isn't this a major catastrophe? You have to come right away and help save a life. Please?"

I soothed the panicking woman and asked for the patient's date of birth before beginning the *songobi*. Suddenly, a flash of light burst across my eyes as if I had been slapped. Out of nowhere, I felt a sharp, shredding pain in the pit of my lower abdomen, and my body shriveled with numbness. Caught off guard by this unexpected pain, I couldn't think straight. I clutched my low stomach and wandered around the room. I saw a vision of a lingering ghost of a family member who had been shot to death, whose sorrow and rage made the spirit unable to move on, hovering above Kim's head.

"*Ajumai*, go quickly and prepare rice cakes. We must conduct a *gosa*[83] and an exorcism ritual to help him recover. Best to leave soon, as I'll also feel better once you're gone."

"Wow, there are some wild ghosts out there." The woman looked at me wide-eyed, but after a series of exclamations, she left. As soon as she did, as if by magic, my stomach pain disappeared. No more than five minutes passed before the woman returned and pushed open the door once again.

"How should I make the rice cakes? Shouldn't you come over in the evening and offer your prayers to bless it?"

---

83. 고사, a ritual including food offerings and prayers to ancestors to dispel misfortune and invite blessings into a family.

She took me in, now perfectly fine, with a puzzled expression and asked, "You weren't feigning illness just now?"

Even I had doubts about the peculiar incident unfolding in such a short time. It seemed as though, in an instant, I had received all that I needed to know about Kim's condition. I instructed the woman to prepare one slab of red bean *tteok*,[84] two slabs of steamed white *tteok*, rice, three colors of *namul*, and pollack and yellow corvina fish with their heads intact by five o'clock.

Around five o'clock, I went to the house the woman had mentioned. The young patient, Kim, laughed while spewing incoherently, clacking his tongue, and behaving nonsensically. I prepared the altar table, rang the gong, and began the invocation.

"Oh, Mountain God of Kim's ancestral land, Village God of this neighborhood here, Guardian Gods of the surrounding mountains and hills, today we offer up our sincere hearts and pray for the healing of Kim's illness this hour and minute."

At that very moment, right after the concluding words of the invocation, I heard the sounds of mocking and snorting sneers from nearby.

"Go ahead and try," the voice jeered. "You will see I won't come out so easily. Pfft!"

In even greater distress than before, the patient groaned, uttering incomprehensible words.

"Should we have taken him to the hospital?" one of the family members sighed. "What are we to do?" Upon hearing this, I suddenly felt drained of energy.

During moments like this, I felt so much regret and pity for myself for choosing the life of a shaman. I mourned over my living in such a manner, praying for other people's peace and well-being while still feeling like I was somehow at fault for others' suffering,

---

84. 떡, a Korean rice cake.

always filled with anxiety and fearing other people's judgment. I struck the gong for a long while, pouring out my deepest heartfelt intentions, yet Kim showed no signs of improvement.

I urgently sent someone home to fetch my Shamanic robes and instruments. After deciding to perform a full-scale *gut*, hanging the Kims' home with deity paintings, I realized there was no one to play the *janggu* drums. As I paced back and forth, feeling lost, friends from the patient's hometown came forward to help.

"How can we find musicians at such a late hour? Why don't we just do it ourselves?" they offered. "We will strike the *janggu* and the *jing*, and you, as the *manshin*, can perform your dance."

With only a meager offering of barley rice and a clumsy setup of *janggu* drums, even the ghosts must have found our display quite absurd. Having no other choice, I donned my ritual robe and held up the rattle, calling the patient's friends to try. Our performance was entirely out of sync. When I instructed them to play only the *janggu*, the men became excited and vigorously struck the drums and gongs. I didn't know whether to laugh or cry. In any case, I raised my fan and rattle high, gathering my heart in earnest devotion.

"O Divine Spirit, ancestral spirits, wandering ghosts who have eagerly awaited this gut, even though our performance may seem like child's play, please graciously bear witness and receive our humble offering. As the saying goes, true devotion springs from sincerity, and sincerity moves the heavens. We beseech the divine and ancestral spirits, who have patiently waited with their hands upon Kim's head, to unite and help remove the affliction plaguing him.

Release him from the grip of malevolent spirits and energies that hover above him, absolve him of his ancestors' sins, and cleanse any impurities he may have acquired from the mountains. Purge and dispel all ailments, much like the dissipating mist and clouds on sacred mountains, the washing away of dirt in the Han River, and the cleansing of soil and sediment from a watermelon.

Infuse vitality into his weary body, deepen his slumber, invigorate his appetite, grant flight to his steps, regulate his temperature, untie and dissolve the knots of illness one by one. Harmonize and pacify the myriad influences of ghosts through your divine intervention."

After saying the prayer, I began to dance, but the *janggu* and *jing* were out of sync, producing a cacophony of sound and making our display barely recognizable as a *gut*. Nevertheless, I vigorously swung the Warrior General deity's swords and danced intensely. When the time came to strip away the lingering spirits from the patient's body, we forced Kim to sit up, and I began to rebuke the spirits.

"Evil spirits, you accursed ghosts! When I address and summon you, come forth immediately! Come out while there's still time, feast upon our prepared offerings, and release your *han* to the beat of drums and gongs. If you refuse, your senses will be starved, your skin will be cut, your bones will be shaved, and a talisman made from scarlet minerals will bind you and cast you into an eternal limbo. Come out now!"

After removing the lingering ghost, I removed the ancestral cloth and sacred sash from the top of the patient's head. Then, I raised the patient's face and sprinkled him with cold water several times before having him lie down again.

After performing a few more *gut* passages, I effortlessly channeled the divine words of *gongsu*: "Yes, don't you worry, don't you fret. Before you know it, the patient will regain his right mind as if he had never been sick. A resentful ghost who passed away before childbirth, a soldier who was killed on the battlefield, and other hungry ghosts who entered him will all be satisfied and cared for by the ancestral spirits. Do not worry and be at peace."

"Yes, please, just get well. That's all we desire."

My neighbor *Ajumai* kept rubbing her hands together in prayer. I poured a drink and sprinkled it over my head before quickly dozing off. Having strongly exerted myself to perform the ritual despite its offbeat rhythm, I was bone tired. Sweat soaked my entire body, drenching even my outer garment as if I had taken a bath.

How much time had passed?

Eventually, the patient slowly rose and sat up. He appeared as undisturbed as someone who had just naturally awakened from sleep.

"Where's my bag? Quickly, hand it to me. I'm in a hurry."

When asked where he was planning to go, he replied that he had made plans with a friend and was running late, looking all around him. His family members thought he was looking for a bag and exchanged glances, signaling to help him find it.

When asked which bag he was looking for, he said he and his friend had put money from a savings bank in the bag. He began searching for his friend, Ki-Seop.

"I'm here. Have you still not awakened from sleep?" asked Ki-Seop, the friend who had played the *janggu* drum, smiling.

"I don't know." Kim looked at Ki-Seop and shook his head in confusion.

"When did this *gut* start? I need to eat. I am hungry."

Then he tapped his forehead with his fist a few times before approaching the altar and taking a seat. It seemed as if he had no memory of being ill or possessed. After serving some rice to the patient, the *gut* ceremony resumed. The unresponsive and possessed patient was now awakened and well, and the *gut* transformed into a festive celebration.

"Hey, isn't it usually women who play the *janggu*? Shouldn't I wear a headscarf?" Ki-Seop, still playing the *janggu*, playfully placed a cloth on his head and convincingly imitated a woman.

Everyone was filled with excitement and danced, their shoulders swaying. The *janggu* and *jing*, though still quite uncoordinated, were played enthusiastically until the very end.

"I played some *janggu*, and so I earned some rice cakes!" the young men bantered.

"*Manshin nuna*, since I played the *jing*, I must be given a big prize." We faced each other and shared a joyous laugh.

The next morning, Kim personally brought the *jing* and the *janggu* home. He paid his respects by bowing at my shrine and expressed his thanks to me. I was simply happy and grateful that he regained his senses and returned to life.

This *gut*, carried out like a child's play without proper musicians or formalities, was accepted by the gods because of our sincere hearts. Is this why it is said that sincerity moves the heavens? I wonder where those friends are now, who didn't hesitate to play the *janggu* and *jing* to save their friend's life. It was an experience I will never forget in my lifetime.

FIFTEEN

What is Your Occupation?

I moved to Seoul after selling my small house in Bupyeong that I had bought for 80,000 *won*. In Seoul, I moved around from one rental to another. During those years, I faced many challenges as a *mudang*. Whenever a *gut* was about to take place, I would feel excitement and joy in my heart, but I also worried about performing it in my tiny, rented room. Anytime I set up a simple ancestral altar and was about to begin the *gut*, the old landlady would start complaining.

"Hey, *mudang*! The floor will break. Can't you see that the floor is going to cave in? Stop jumping, stop!"

If a customer were to use the restroom, she would stand outside the door, complaining and yelling.

"Hey there! Why are you using someone else's bathroom? It's going to overflow. Get out now!"

No guest liked having their time in the bathroom interrupted by banging and clamoring outside. I loathed her nitpicking, but I could say nothing to her. Even now, landlords don't like renting space to *mudangs*, so back then, I felt I had to be grateful to have any room at all. But I began cleaning the restroom and paid the electric and water bills I was asked to pay, and soon, the complaints and disagreements stopped.

The first place my mother and I settled down after moving to Seoul was Noryangjin. We packed a few bundles onto a truck and moved somewhere we didn't know a single soul. Our belongings were so shabby that people would have thought we were headed to a junk shop. That first space was a small two-room dwelling, where my mother occupied the larger and more comfortable room while I took the smaller one. The days were bitterly cold, and we survived on just a single coal briquette per day. Even when guests came, the space remained cold. Visitors who came to have their fortunes read clicked their tongues, asking what kind of *mudang* doesn't even have a cushion to sit on?

"I have to hurry home. I might freeze to death while getting my fortune!" the guests waiting their turn complained.

But when word spread about the accuracy of my divinations, I started having a steady stream of customers. After performing several *guts* in the neighborhood, I even became friendly with some neighbors. Among them, Young-Gil's mother recommended that I join her *gye*[85] group, a traditional money fund. Although I was barely making ends meet, I considered that the lump sum from the *gye* would allow me to move to a better rental, so I decided to commit.

---

85. 계, a traditional Korean money-saving tradition with a long history. A group of people would agree to contribute a fixed amount of money every month to a common pool, and the pooled money was distributed monthly to one of the participants in rotation, allowing each person to receive a lump sum once during the designated *gye* period. The agreement was done on good faith with no contract or legal authority, and there were incidents of loss and theft, yet it is a tradition that showcases the faith and mutual aid Korean people have had for one another.

We were already poor, and contributing to a 50,000 *won gye* made our living even more precarious. Our evening meals consisted of bean sprout or kimchi porridge with wild greens—and even those could hardly be called proper porridge, as there were only a few grains of rice in each. Clutching our hunger-addled stomachs, I diligently poured money into the *gye*.

Several months passed, and fall arrived. The long-awaited day for my turn to receive the *gye* money finally arrived, but I didn't receive any contact from the *gye* leader. Unable to wait any longer, I rushed to her house, and she sent me home, promising to come by the next day. True to her word, she arrived the following day with the money wrapped in a bundle. I confirmed that it was indeed 50,000 *won*.

After eating a slice of the pear I had served, she searched my face and began speaking. "Look here. What if I gave you a bigger interest if you let me borrow this now?"

I had already planned to sign a rental contract with the money, so I couldn't take her offer. Yet the woman simply grabbed the money back, stuffed it in her skirt, and stood up to leave. She said it was protocol for her to give me the money in front of other *gye* members, so I had to follow her.

Being naïve and ignorant about the ways of the world, I followed the woman and waited for a long time outside another house. The woman didn't emerge during my long wait, and when I briefly went to the bathroom, she disappeared, wearing someone else's shoes. I searched for her for three days, but it was all in vain.

I confided what happened to me to a man I knew, Mr. Soo-Young, who took me to the Noryangjin police station. The detective who listened to my story instructed me to provide false information.

"Don't say she left when you went to the bathroom; instead,

say she ran away. That way, we can report it as theft and misappropriation of funds."

"But that house didn't have a back door," I replied.

The detective looked at me as if I were pathetic.

"Who's going to verify the details?" he said. "What matters is that you get your money back."

I followed his recommendation and composed a statement. Sometime later, a court summons arrived. I went to the police station with Mr. Soo-Young and appeared for questioning. Even though I hadn't committed any wrongdoing, I felt intimidated. The investigator interrogated me with a stern and unyielding voice.

"Ms. Kim, you claim to have accompanied her, so how can it be considered theft? Moreover, the house doesn't even have a back door, so how could she have escaped through the back?"

I had naively followed the detective's instructions regarding my written statement but could not speak lies aloud. If I revealed the circumstances surrounding the "back door" story, it could harm the detective who helped me prepare the statement, so I couldn't speak the truth. However, it was the next question that silenced me completely.

"What is your occupation?"

"I…"

I hesitated and couldn't bring myself to say "*mudang*." The money I had painstakingly saved, enduring cold and hunger, as if collecting ant eggs one by one, was ruthlessly snatched away in one swoop. While the *gye* leader was caught by the police and released within a day, I could not receive my rightful money due to the "back door" story concocted by the police detective.

It was unfair that my money was stolen from me, but what felt even more heartbreaking was how pitiful and miserable I found myself, unable to confidently say "*mudang*" when asked about my occupation. It left a lasting scar on my heart.

A *mudang* is a disciple of Divine Spirit who sees beyond this world but is often clumsy and naïve in the human realm. Perhaps that's why some people look down upon and try to deceive *mudangs* from time to time.

Once, a monk entered through the door of our shabby rental home. He joined his palms together and recited the mantras of Buddha and Bodhisattva, and I put my palms together in response.

"What brings you here?" I asked.

"*Bosal-nim,*[86] I have come to collect offerings and light candles to pray for the numerous soldiers who have been dispatched to Vietnam and are suffering injuries and casualties. Please consider donating."

Without uttering a word, I handed over a box of candles and a small sum of money. About three days later, the monk returned.

"When I lit the candles you gave me last time, they initially emitted a brilliant iridescent light, but it soon blackened and dimmed out."

Uncertain of how to respond, I simply looked at the monk.

"When the chief monk asked who donated the candles and I mentioned you, he instructed me to quickly go and relay to you that you must stay home and not go out."

I nearly broke out in laughter at his words, but I bit my lower lip and asked, "So what should I do then?"

"We must pray for you, of course."

The monk asked for a gold necklace or ring. He said he also needed three handfuls of rice and a thread to set them on a high place while performing his prayer ritual. All that was required for me to do, he said, was bow. I called for Spirit quietly in my mind.

---

86. 보살님, a respectful way Buddhists refer to a female devotee.

"*Shinryeong-nim*, please look at this person sitting before me."

No matter how I observed him, it was clear that he was a con man.

Should I report him? Should I persuade him? I wondered. If I succeeded in talking sense to him, that would be fortunate, but I worried he might try to harm me. Deciding to entrust everything to Great Spirit, I told the monk to return the next day. When the monk returned the next day, I led him to my shrine inside the house. The monk seemed startled as he entered and saw the Shamanic shrine. With a low, firm voice, I reprimanded him.

"Look here. When you first came by, I gave you candles to light and even offered you a small sum. Regardless of how you use what I gave, whether you light the candles or not, I considered it an offering to Buddha, trusting that Buddha will see my heart. However, how could you, dressed in the sacred monk's robe, go around and con others? I am just a humble *mudang*, but please understand that I'm relaying the words of Divine Spirit. With these divine words, I would be thankful if you repent and become a good person living an honest life. I don't know what you plan to do, but I know that spilled water cannot be gathered, and wrongdoing cannot be undone. It is not too late to change your ways. Perhaps in the distant future, after you change your ways, you will look back on this moment as a good event."

The monk's face turned red with embarrassment. He bowed his head several times and repeatedly thanked me.

"I have met a good person like you in this harsh world," he said. "I will take your wise words to heart and become a good person. I promise to visit you again in the future. You have saved me today."

The man bowed respectfully and left. I was grateful that he

received my words with such grace. I couldn't help but wonder if it was not the will of Divine Spirit for the man to have come to my home. Perhaps Spirit, who blesses those on the right path, felt compassion for someone who had strayed and wanted to open a new direction for him. It led me to reflect even further on the profound and expansive nature of Spirit.

SIXTEEN

A *Mudang* is Subject to Eradication

There was a time when it was extremely difficult to perform a *gut*. During the New Village Movement of the 1970s, *mudangs* and *guts* were dismissed as mere superstitions, and I found my tradition being driven out and myself chased away. Perhaps this movement led to replacing thatched roofs with slate ones in rural homes, but I cannot deny my sorrow and regret that the movement caused the extinction of our Shamanic traditions and the spirit connections passed down by our ancestors.

Even during these dire times, occasional rituals still occurred in and around Seoul. Homes that requested *guts* treated me like a fugitive, hiding me away. While they rushed to welcome me into their homes, they also tried very hard to avoid being noticed or heard by others, and we conducted the rituals as quietly as possible. If, by any chance, a report was filed with the authorities, it would result in a huge commotion. Police were dispatched, turning the sacred setting of a *gut* into a scene of raging chaos.

"*Mudang,* come out! Bring your *janggu* and come out quickly!" Just like a cow being dragged to the slaughterhouse, I was forcibly dragged to the police station, where I had to beg forgiveness and even write statements of apology.

One day, a *gut* was scheduled in a small rural village. I was accompanied there by the household's grandmother, who had requested the *gut,* carrying the necessary items for the ritual. As we passed the police station, the grandmother was so nervous that she started behaving unnaturally. She would take a step, then glance towards the police station, take another step, and hurriedly turn to look towards the police station again. Following behind her erratic footsteps, I sensed that something might happen. Sure enough, the police officer who observed her suspicious behavior called the grandmother and stopped her.

She could have acted calmly, but instead, overcome with fear, she started babbling. "*Aigo,* I don't know anything!" she cried before fleeing.

Of course, she was quickly caught. As the police officer grabbed her belongings, the Shamanic instruments and ritual tools spilled out and rolled on the ground.

"Oh my, I don't know anything. Really! I'm innocent." The grandmother was scared stiff and out of her mind. "I only did what that woman over there told me to do."

The police officer's gaze turned towards me. I collected myself and tried to stay calm, knowing I could make the situation worse or better. It is said that even when caught by a tiger, you can survive if you keep a clear mind.

"Those are Shamanic garments worn during a *gut*; what I have on my head is just rice and rice cakes," I said. "If you excuse us just this once, I will be more careful."

I spoke politely and humbly, willing myself to not give in

and plead instead. The police officer looked me up and down. His eyes were full of eager excitement as if he had just caught a serious criminal.

"You people going around performing stupid *guts* during these times. *Mudangs* are subject to eradication!" he said. "Don't you know we have a directive to eliminate all the outdated shrines and customs? What mess is all this? Senselessly slaughtering pigs, too. You women must be detained for a few days to come to your senses."

The old lady clung to the police officer's pants as if her life depended on it and begged. "*Aigo*, if my son finds out, he'll kick me out of the house. Please have mercy. Please look the other way just this once."

On that particular day, I could no longer hold back my anger. I could no longer bear the constant begging, pleading, and wretched clinging whenever a *mudang* was caught honoring ancient traditions. All the rage I had bottled up inside finally surged to the top of my head.

"Fine, do as you please," I said. "In these hard times when making a living is so difficult, if you want to lock us up and feed us for a few months, that's fine with me. Go right ahead."

I also spoke my mind to the old lady, still pleading desperately. "Grandmother, what crime did you commit? Why are you begging and making a ruckus? Did we rob a bank? Did we break into somebody's home in the middle of the night to steal?"

I came on strong, and the police officer, who had just been threatening us, flinched. But I didn't stop there and kept pouring out the rest of my words at him.

"Don't you have parents? The *gut* is something our ancestors, our grandmothers, used to do. When the hospitals fail and medicine doesn't work, they turn to a *gut*. How can a *mudang* refuse them? Also, if we do something wrong, we should face the law and not be scolded by you. What gives you the right to speak impolitely to an elder? You should be ashamed!"

"Impolite? No, well yes..." mumbled another police officer standing nearby. Just then, someone else came over. With our vibrant clothes and a pork leg rolling on the ground, we were a sight that needed no explanation. Even then, I couldn't contain my anger and was huffing and puffing, "You're scolding us for nothing!"

Upon seeing me, the man who had just arrived said, "Hurry, let them go."

Then, to me, "Hey, if you have plenty of pork legs, give us one and leave."

I handed over a pork leg without uttering a word and hurriedly left, taking my belongings. Even upon returning home, my heart couldn't find peace. On the one hand, I was satisfied that I had said everything I wanted to say, but on the other hand, I was bothered by thoughts of how much longer I might be able to live the life of a *mudang*. Yet, I knew I only had one path in front of me—a path that required me to tread a long and solitary journey alone. Even after that incident, there were countless more times that the *gut* I was performing was forcefully stopped, and I was dragged to a police station.

After relocating to Seokgwan-dong, I had to endure yet another ordeal with the police during a *Mansudaetak-gut*.

My house in Seokgwan-dong had a powerful energy. Shortly after moving there, I had a vivid dream: in the middle of the kitchen, a clean-cut and handsome young man was bathing. The bathwater was grimy and overflowing onto the floor. When I asked why he wasn't hurrying out of the kitchen, he smiled and said, "I am trying to help you here." It was a dream showing that Divine Spirit had already arrived at the house before us.

When I opened my eyes, I discovered it was just a dream. I could hear the wind blowing outside. When I went out to look at the night sky, two shooting stars traveled overhead from the direction of the old house to my new home. It felt auspicious. A few days later, I got the call to perform a big *gut*.

Mansudaetak was a *gut* traditionally performed in noble homes. The ritual satirized the current world and was intended to wish longevity for household elders and those who enter the realm of bliss following their deaths. Such an elaborate offering could only be held with the help of my regulars.

On the day the *gut* began, many guests arrived from different places. A cow and two pigs were sacrificed. The large, decorated banner lanterns, ritual money, and paintings of the Seven Star God[87] and Emperor God were displayed before the ritual started. However, only moments after the drumbeats began, a police car arrived. The officers caused an uproar outside and called for me to come out.

The hosts of the *gut* rushed inside, their faces pale with fear. "Hey, you need to escape. Hurry! Hurry!" One urged me out with a panicked voice.

But I was almost numb with calmness.

"We can't hold a *gut* like this. The fist comes first before the law."

While the host and I struggled back and forth about the best course of action, I suddenly heard a yell from my sworn brother Man-Young Kim, who had been dancing the Gangryeong mask dance[88] outside with my mother. Motivated by all the commotion, the host moved a low round table to the window and pushed me onto it. I found myself stepping onto the round table and climbing

---

87. 칠성신, also called *Chilseong-shin*.

88. 강령탈춤, a traditional mask dance from Gangryeong area of Hwanghae province, was designated as Intangible Cultural Property in 1970.

out the window. I climbed to the neighboring house and crouched beside the earthenware pots stored outside.

Had even an hour passed?

Finally, a signal came indicating that it was safe to return inside. The house was in chaotic disarray. It seemed that my mother had confronted the police officers who had forcefully entered, pushing and pulling in a struggle. Refusing to let go of the policeman's waist, she was kicked down the stairs and had been taken to the hospital. The *manshin* from Pyongyang continued the *gut* after the new *manshin* was arrested by the police. Then the new *manshin* was arrested instead of me. However, we couldn't halt a *gut* that had already begun. A *gut* required a leader, so I had to continue the ceremony. The *Mansudaetak-gut* lasts for five nights and six days, and facing such trouble on the very first day was no ordinary matter. It was a grave situation.

Two days later, another police officer arrived. Man-Young Kim asked why the police had returned after they had already arrested someone, but his protest was in vain. I needed to go to the station to resolve the matter myself.

At the police station, I found the young couple who had complained, stating that they couldn't live with the noise of drumming and gongs beginning at dawn. They'd requested that I be punished.

As I entered the station, I quickly bowed my head. "First of all, I am sorry. I apologize with all due respect."

I offered a standing bow to the young couple, almost touching the ground with my nose. "I understand it must be difficult, but please allow us to continue. The noise will only last for a short while longer."

"By 'a short while,' until when?" the woman asked, her eyes narrowing in discontent.

I was cautious in my reply, "Until the day after tomorrow."

I observed her reaction. The woman's mouth fell open, and she quickly jerked her head away from me.

"Please resolve this immediately. I can't take it anymore!"

Strangely, I felt a sense of relief and calmness. The man accompanying the woman chimed in, urging us to finish quickly.

After leaving the police station, I visited my disciple, who was detained on my behalf. It was almost ten o'clock in the morning when I was finally permitted to see her. The new *manshin* smiled at me from behind the bars.

"Ah, how come you're in there as if you've committed a crime? It should be me in that place, not you." I burst into tears, overwhelmed by the guilt I felt towards the student suffering in my place and the resentment and sorrow that arose from this inexplicable situation that labeled us criminals and sinners. I wailed for a long time in front of my student. The only thing I could do was pay her fine and bring her back with me.

The following day, the police charged into the *gut* yet again. Our efforts to muffle the sounds of the gong and drums proved futile. We finally gave up on performing the *gut* at the home and relocated to Samgak Mountain. We settled into a house at the mountaintop, next to Ilsunsa Temple.

Since my elderly mother suffered from asthma and couldn't climb the mountain, several people took turns carrying her on their backs. As I held her, my mother commented that she found my back the most comfortable.

"I never knew how high you had to climb..." she said.

Over the remaining two nights and three days, we successfully completed the *gut*, vigorously playing the *janggu* and *jing* to our heart's content. This *Mansudaetak-gut* had been eventful and truly unforgettable.

Regardless of what others say, I am a *mudang*. I have traversed the winding and treacherous path of the spirit world, stumbling upon rocky terrain and falling onto countless muddy paths. In my younger days, I resented and blamed the gods for allowing me to suffer so much pain. However, as I persevered through these challenges, I emerged stronger and more determined. Perhaps the hardships and trials were all part of the divine plan to forge and fortify me.

SEVENTEEN

Why Did You Have to Leave Us Like That?

My younger brother, Joong-Hyun, is the sibling to whom I have shown the most affection, or *jeong*. Since he was a newborn, he practically grew up on my back, and even as an adult, he listened to me. Although he got married and had four children, I always felt sorry for him as he struggled to make ends meet through his work as a welder.

When Joong-Hyun turned thirty-two, he wanted to build a house. Around the same time, our mother planned to get dental implants ahead of her 60th birthday celebration. I suggested it best to build a house or get dental work done during auspicious years. But my mother thought otherwise. She had consulted Old Man Oh from our hometown, who was famous for his *I Ching* divinations. He checked the auspicious and inauspicious signs and concluded that building a house or celebrating her sixtieth birthday was fine and was rather offended that I disapproved. Despite my reluctance, I accommodated my mother's wishes—even though she was already displeased with me and often expressed her anger. Joong-Hyun also went ahead with his plan to build a new house.

My mother turned sixty on the eighth day of the tenth Lunar month. It was a bitterly cold winter, with temperatures dropping as low as minus 17 degrees Celsius. I made an offering of the meticulously prepared food my younger brother had sent to my shrine and prayed for my mother's health and longevity.

"May my mother be blessed for the next three years, filled with grace and ease, and may my brother's new home and the ensuing three years be free from any obstacles or hardship. Please continue to guide and assist us as we trust and rely on Divine Spirit."

However, during the prayer, I started jumping up and down frantically. *How dare you defy the will of Spirit?* chastened a voice in my mind. *You're a disgrace! What will you do if calamitous winds blow and hailstorms pour down in the next three years? How dare you offend the gods?*

My body trembled as if struck by lightning. After a while, I managed to calm down, but I felt uneasy facing my younger brother. I packed the feast and set off to my mother's home in Bupyeong. My brother, still facing financial difficulties, was wearing a suit and shaking noticeably. There were already many guests at my mother's place, and the aroma of food being prepared filled the air.

Upon arriving, I felt a bit ashamed for having initially opposed hosting a celebratory feast for her *60th hwangap* celebration, which only comes once in a lifetime. My mother had struggled and devoted all her energy to raising my siblings and me after becoming widowed at age thirty-seven. I offered a glass to my mother and tried my best to make her shine and stand out.

In the end, my mother had her celebration, and my brother built a new house the following year. My mother still seemed displeased with me, showing signs of being upset over the most minor things. One day, when I returned home after an outing, I discovered that my mother had left our shared home without saying a word to me and gone to live with my brother. The wardrobe was cleared of her clothes, devoid and empty. I felt sad and upset.

About a month later, I received word that my mother was very ill. Upon hearing the news, I immediately rushed to my brother's home, taking the first train at dawn. When I arrived, I found my mother on her sickbed, muttering, "No, don't die. Can't die." An ominous feeling swept over me as I saw my brother, also sick, lying at her feet.

That night, I had a dream in which I was facing off with a man in a sword fight. A woman and another man were standing nearby. I felt like I could kill my opponent with a single stab. As I looked at the man and was about to ask him to yield, I saw him take his giant sword and pierce the man on the sideline. I woke up absolutely startled. Even though it was just a dream, I felt extremely unsettled.

Lost in deep thought about the dream, I fell asleep and dreamed again. This time, the dream took place in a rundown house with white plaster walls, empty of people. Only my mother was there, rummaging through old clothes, searching for something. I was wearing a worn-out straw shoe with just the sole intact, searching for the other shoe. Once again, it was an ominous dream.

When I returned to my brother's home the day after the dream, my brother was awake. I bought a chicken, changed my mother's clothes, counted sixty-two grains of rice to place in my mother's mouth, and then made her spit them out before stuffing them into the chicken's mouth.

"I am planning on doing a *gut* on the new Lunar month," I announced. "Here, I transfer my mother's fate into this chicken and sacrifice it through *daesudaemyeong*.[89] Please help her recover so that she can participate in the Lunar New Year ritual."

After offering the prayer, I buried the chicken alongside my mother's old clothes in the front yard, instructing my brother not to look behind him and to return home via a different path. Then I returned to my home. Three days later, I received an urgent call from my mother informing me that my brother was very ill. She urged me to come prepared for a *gut*. I grabbed my bundle of sacred tools and hurried over. As I opened the gate and entered, I noticed my older sister coming out to the yard with a bundle of rice cakes. She walked strangely, like she was feeling her way with her feet on the ground and couldn't find the floor to step inside the house. When I asked her why, she chuckled and said her vision had suddenly gone black.

My brother had also gotten very sick about two or three years before. Back then, thanks to the *gut*, he recovered and regained his strength without needing to go to the hospital. This time, however, I had a foreboding feeling that the *gut* wouldn't work. My brother's complexion had darkened. His lips were blackened and dry, and his breath was as shallow as if it would evaporate into the sky.

"What to do? Oh, what to do ..."

A despairing sigh escaped from me. I pulled out the pin I had placed in my clothes and attempted to pierce my brother's hand in various places, but no blood spilled out. We couldn't even try to perform a *gut*. We just hailed a taxi and went straight to the hospital.

"*Aigo*, what are we going to do? Please don't die. You can't die. Don't die."

The taxi driver scolded us for bringing bad luck into his cab by crying. My brother, who was already unconscious, died as soon

---

89. 대수대명, a Shamanic practice transferring one's fate and/or burdens to another, often to a living animal, such as a chicken, before sacrificing it.

as we arrived at the hospital; his death the result of lying at my mother's sickbed. My brother was only thirty-four-years-old. He left behind four pitiable children, including a nursing baby. How could he close his eyes and leave behind these young ones? After burying my brother, who had endured such a harsh and short life, my footsteps remained rooted in the cold ground, unable to move on for a long while.

EIGHTEEN

Many Mouths to Feed, Maybe I Should Give Business a Try?

After my brother's death, my mother and I took a long while to recover. I found it hard to go out and see young people. How could my brother leave this world so suddenly at such a young age when so many others were living healthy and happy lives? The winter when my brother died was exceptionally snowy: would he be able to find peace under the cold ground, leaving behind such young children?

Eventually, spring came. One morning, I woke up at 5:30 and opened the window, and there, perched on the eaves, was a swallow that used to arrive at the same time each day. I exchanged words with that bird as if it were my brother.

By this time, I had moved yet again, now to Sando-dong in Seoul. Whenever my mother visited me, her steps seemed weary. She didn't speak of it, but she seemed to see her absent son every-where. Whenever I had some money, I visited my mother in Bupyeong, but returning home alone felt heavy. As my mother was suffering from severe asthma, I thought it best to bring her to live with me in Seoul again. She had lived with me even when her son was alive, and now that he had departed this world, it seemed even more appropriate.

I rented a taxi and brought my mother to my home in Seoul. The taxi traveled smoothly on the recently built Gyeongin Expressway. I talked about the new expressway with her, hoping to distract her from her grief even for a moment. After some time, I also brought my nephews and nieces to my home. Since losing their father, they were like kites with the strings cut off. The youngest, Mi-Kyoung, who hadn't even turned one yet, brought her blanket and clung to my hand when I said, "Let's go to grand-mother's." These poor little children were so impoverished and neglected that their faces were swollen with mumps.

Several people lived in my home: the young children, my elderly mother, and myself. The number of mouths to feed tripled overnight, adding to my anxiety about money. The New Village Movement had gained momentum, making it even more challenging to perform *guts*. In the past, our preparations for the fall and winter seasons included simply making soybean paste, preparing kimchi, and observing ancestral rites. But now, things were more complicated. To perform a ritual, we had to talk with the local police station and the community association and seek understanding from our neighbors.

Making ends meet became harder and harder. Summer passed, but things didn't get better in the fall. Packing lunchboxes for three school-aged children became a challenge. Recognizing the dire state of our family, the neighborhood association arranged for us to receive flour rations. Our dinners were *sujebi*[90] soup, which often served as our lunches, too. There were many days when

---

90. 수제비, a soup of clear broth and hand-torn flour dumplings.

sujebi became our only meal, three times a day. We barely had enough to feed everyone. If we were fortunate enough to have left-over cold rice, we would add a lot of water, boil it down to a watery rice soup, and serve one bowl for everyone to share.

In the time it took me to go in and out of the kitchen serving everyone their soup, the children finished everything I had given them and were scraping their empty bowls. Still famished, some sucked on their spoons and eyed my bowl. I would give each a spoonful from my bowl, and then I would be left with just clear broth to eat.

Clothing all the children was also a problem. I dressed them in old and used clothes I collected from my regular customers. My mother and I mended and altered them to fit, but they were hardly shapely or appealing. Nevertheless, we were grateful that we had clothes to wear. During winter, we worried about keeping warm. Whenever we changed the charcoal briquettes, we tried to seal the holes in them as much as possible to prolong the heat. I would check on the coal several times throughout the night, afraid of missing the right time to change it and being left in the freezing cold.

I spent my days feeding the children out of what little groceries we could afford, doing laundry for the family, and once in a long while, when a customer came by, I performed divination for them. Every day was a drain and a struggle; my heart felt like it was shriveling up. If someone had opened my chest to look at my heart, it would have been a burnt lump of coal. I often sobbed with exhaustion, and there were times when my teary eyes made it difficult to see the holes in the charcoal briquette as I changed it.

As winter deepened and the Lunar New Year approached, my number of customers gradually increased, and I managed to save a little money. Tired of barely scraping by each day and constantly worrying about providing for the children, I contemplated other options for earning a living.

One day, my niece came home from school with a sullen face and said, "*Gomo*, the kids are teasing me, calling me a *mudang's* child."

"A *mudang's* child?"

"Yeah, they keep teasing me and hitting me, saying that their mom told them not to play with a *mudang's* kid."

Something hot rose inside me. A *mudang* is not a criminal or someone spreading diseases. We don't cause harm; rather, we do all we can to help. I couldn't understand why we were still so ostracized and hated.

I felt my heart hardening with determination and resentment. *Okay, fine. I will live differently now*, I thought to myself. *I won't lose to them all.*

I decided to try my hand at business that summer. An acquaintance I knew suggested running a summer stall at a nearby beach on Deokjeok Island. I was told that I could turn quite a profit for just a single season's work. I needed the money, but more than that, I wanted to offer my nieces and nephews, who had limited opportunities to explore the world, a chance to enjoy the ocean.

With the money I'd saved all the winter, I set up a small shop at Deokjeok Island Beach. I took the leap because an acquaintance agreed to lend a hand. I hired a cook and a helper, then sold food and drinks like *seolleongtang*[91] soup, beer, and other snacks. Given this was my first business venture, it was far from easy. I woke up at two o'clock every morning and headed to Incheon to buy supplies. By 6 a.m., I would board the ferry with my goods in tow. By the time I got back, it was already around 11:00 in the

---

91. 설렁탕, a soup with beef bone and meat, served with rice.

morning—I don't know how I found the additional strength to carry the heavy loads of beer or blocks of ice on my head, walking from the dock to my shop. By the time I unloaded the goods, I felt utterly drained, as if my entire body were waterlogged.

At the stall, I spent the entire day darting around like a squirrel, tending to my business. I worked ten times harder than anyone else, tirelessly running around and staying open much later than other shops. Yet I didn't make any profit. Even as summer was ending and the beach was emptied of vacationers, things didn't change. I was crushed. I even got into a fight when I discovered the person who had promised to help me had been stealing my customers for another shop. I was angry and sad, having been betrayed by someone I had trusted so much.

Trying to console myself, I took a few drinks of alcohol, making me both drunk and sick. I spent the night throwing up, and by dawn, my hands and feet were ice cold, and my entire body started convulsing. I was discovered by someone taking a night stroll and taken to the hospital. My spirit daughter Ok-Ja came and tried to prick my fingertips with a needle, but it was useless.

"I am going to die in this unfamiliar place," I told her. "What will happen to the children?"

Even as I tried to speak, my tongue stiffened, and I could not utter a word. After receiving treatment at the hospital, I could only return home after resting at Ok-Ja's house in Incheon for another day. My youngest sister, who received the news of my illness, came right away and burst into tears upon seeing my face. Even I was shocked by my appearance. I was nothing but skin and bones, gaunt and haggard.

My sister managed to find enough money for me to take a taxi back home to Seoul. Despite having some rice gruel and lying down, I felt desolate and overwhelmed. The future seemed bleak and insurmountable. I was torn between the decision to keep living or to just die, my mind wavering back and forth like it was riding a swing.

Then, on what must have been the third day after my illness, a fiery shout suddenly erupted from my mouth.

"Do you still refuse to come to your senses?" it shouted. "Get down on your knees right this minute, beg for forgiveness, and dedicate yourself to Divine Spirit, you wretch!"

Suddenly, my right hand slapped my right cheek hard, like a light flashed before my eyes.

"Do you still insist on following futile thoughts? I will punish you by confining you within your body, rendering you immobile like a chamber pot stuck in a room. You must resist the influence of the lowly ghosts and seek the guidance of Divine Spirit."

I kept shouting at myself and slapping my own cheek. I couldn't raise my head or stand up. I made attempts to get up, but my body refused to straighten. With both hands on the floor, I strained to lift my bottom, but it was in vain. The following morning, at dawn, I awoke and crawled on all fours to the shrine. As I bowed before Divine Spirit, tears welled up.

"Please save me just once," I prayed. "Please think of the help-less children who cry for food when they are hungry. Fearing they would starve, I foolishly thought I could run a business. Please forgive me and have mercy. Please help us."

My tears overflowed like water from a broken dam. Sobbing and wailing, I pleaded with Divine Spirit over and over again.

"Why did I try to leave the path of Divine Spirit? No matter how great the hunger or agony, where will I find solace if I abandon Spirit? I must put an end to foolish thoughts and think about the children. I must live."

I prayed and prayed, rubbing my hands together in earnest.

Once again, a stern voice echoed from my mouth. I was questioning and answering myself, scolding and pleading with myself.

"Have you regained your senses now?"

"Yes."

"I will help you heal the sick and raise up those who are lying down."

A few days later, a customer arrived for the first time in a long while. She was a middle-aged woman who had sought my help because her child was sick. But I had no confidence in my ability to perform divination.

"What do I know about divining? I don't know anything," I muttered.

The woman was so desperate that she opened the shrine door herself and brought out the divination table.

"Please, don't refuse me like this. Please give it a try. It looks like my child is about to die."

But even as I heard about a child on the verge of death, I felt indifference.

I couldn't even save my own brother. How can I help someone else heal? I thought.

My heart was not in it. I almost blurted out my thoughts about losing my brother but held back and sat at the divination table. The woman informed me that her sick child was five years old and gave me their date of birth.

As soon as I heard her words, I found my mouth effortlessly channeling. "It's a malevolent influence from visiting death. It must have followed your husband home from the funeral he attended."

Just a moment before, my heart was unwilling, and I lacked confidence. But as I spoke, those feelings evaporated, and I found myself effortlessly instructing the woman on how to pray and perform the rite for driving out the evil. Even I was surprised at myself.

The next morning, the woman returned to my home carrying a large bag of rice. Even before she entered, she started bowing deeply, thanking me. She had followed my instructions, and after performing the prayer and cleansing rite, her child's condition miraculously improved. The child's swollen belly subsided, and after passing gas, the child asked for food. The woman was overjoyed and kept thanking me.

Inside, I kept silently thanking Spirit.

NINETEEN

Neomse is on TV!

The longer I was a *mudang*, the more I desperately wished to preserve the legacy of our *gut*. I considered how the simple act of our grandparents and ancestors placing a water offering on an earthenware pot and praying for blessings and well-being suddenly became mere superstition? Why did the Japanese, who also worshipped and bowed to spirits at their shrines, accuse the Korean spirits and gods of being superstitions? Why do we Koreans readily look up to and embrace foreign civilizations and cultures yet reject our own traditions?

As I wrestled with such questions, I arrived at a deep desire to embrace the traditional *gut* rituals, preserve them in their original form, and pass them down to future generations.

One day, I went to Incheon to meet Yang So-un, who worked performing the Bongsan Mask Dance. Through Yang's introduction, I came to know a person named Kim Jin-ok. Jin-ok was from Yeonpyeong Island and performed the Gangnyeong Mask Dance.

"Sister, would you like to perform a Yeonpyeong song with me?"

"Why would we do that?" I asked.

"Listen, people are looking for old folk songs again these days."

My ears perked up. I already felt frustrated at seeing the traditions of my hometown dissipate as people resettled in the South after evacuating during the war. It seemed that my desire to preserve our traditions might be fulfilled. After much thought, I made up my mind to sing the Yeonpyeong songs.

That's how I ended up participating in the 1967 National Folk Arts Performance Contest on October 13, 1967.

Despite my tight financial situation, I scraped together savings and bought the necessary props for my performance. The Gangnyeong group presented the Bongsan Mask Dance while I took the stage with a Yeonpyeong song. The National Folk Arts Performance Contest was a prestigious competition that brought together folk art practitioners and experts from all over the country to showcase regional folk performances representing the eight regions of Korea. Those who were part of a large group presentation exuded energy and enthusiasm. I pushed aside the creeping nervousness and trusted that Divine Spirit would be on my side. Once on stage, I felt a sense of strength in my stomach and power in my legs.

> "This Na-na-ni is a mountain. If not to play, then what?
> Little calf, don't get trapped, but play freely.
> This Na-na-ni is a mountain. If not to play, then what?
> Throw the lazy sister where the tigers roam.
> Plant lettuce in the front field, my dancing sister-in-law…"

The Yeonpyeong folk song was traditionally sung by women when their husbands went fishing in the sea. The women would fill a dark earthenware bowl with water, place a basin on top, and strike it with coiled rope and sticks to create a paddling sound while singing this song. I danced barefoot and sang, sounding sorrowful and enchanting. After the song ended, I quickly changed into ritual attire and performed the three-minute *Baeyeonsin-gut* ritual dance.

At the end of the contest, I received an individual award for the Yeonpyeong folk song I'd sung for the first time. The prize money was 30,000 *won*. After winning the award, I received interview requests from all over. My throat tightened as I answered the reporters' questions, causing me to pause. I felt sad, missing my hometown in the North and thinking about the lifelong pain of being rejected as a shaman. If I had been the daughter of a wealthy family, I would have still been at an age of being sheltered and doted on at home. If I were to compare my youth to a flower, at that time, I was still shyly budding, not yet fully bloomed. However, I had experienced so much devastation in my young life that I was like a flower struck by a harsh frost—I had withered. If I thought it had all been a dream, I would have been afraid to close my eyes, fearing that I would relive the nightmare again.

Yet people were now watching me and what I had to offer. When I danced on the stage, the camera focused on me, and there was interest in the folk songs I sang. It felt like another world, like dreaming another kind of dream. It seemed as if Divine Spirit had offered me a healing hand after the prolonged pain I had endured.

The announcement that I'd received an award at the National Folk Arts Performance Contest was made through newspapers and broadcasts. Gradually, my name started to become known throughout the media. Shortly after my performance, the Yeonpyeong folk song was introduced on KBS TV. It was my first-ever television appearance. People from my hometown were delighted, saying, "Neomse has become a star and is on TV!" Some shamans who were jealous switched the channel, calling me a disgrace and a shame. Yet I remained undaunted and gave it my all.

Since I was young, my stubbornness and perseverance set me apart from others. While others would shake their heads in defeat at a complex *gut*, I felt an even stronger desire to perform it. I believed that committing my heart to it was half of the task.

I embraced the notion that if I appeared on TV and faced ridicule or shame, it was my burden to bear. It was with that mindset that I had always made countless commitments to see things through until the very end. Whenever I performed on stage or conducted a *gut*, it felt as if someone was guiding me from above. As a result, my songs and sounds flowed seamlessly, and my dances grew increasingly self-confident.

I continued participating in the National Folk Arts Performance Contest for years to come. Occasionally, I didn't receive an award, but I wasn't disappointed. When the contest was held in Busan, I took part in a performance called *Haejujanggun*, for the Haeju Warrior General. Just like before, the performers of the Bongsan Mask Dance and the Gangnyeong Mask Dance provided me with both material and spiritual support. Thanks to the assistance of many people, I received participation and individual awards.

Despite my success, performing the *jakdu* dance in a location other than an actual *gut* ceremony was still unusual. To perform the *jakdu*, I had to diligently sharpen my blades where nobody could see, which posed a challenge. But I didn't mind. I climbed onto the stage barefoot, danced on the *jakdu* blades, and offered *gongsu* oracles.

"Eh—hey, how delightful and wonderful!
I thought you forgot me and would bury me,
but how did you get smart and invite me here?
It's a joy to be brought back. It's a joy to be with you all.
I am Jakdu Janggun, the divine warrior with twin-star
jakdu blades,
I am magnificent, I am powerful, I am greedy!
With a single strike, I defeat the enemies,
Like a ball, like a pinecone, I play with the Namsan Mountain,
I can tilt the land miles away to drink from its waters,
With a single strike, my enemies fall like autumn leaves ..."

I jumped on the *jakdu* blades, gripping the sacred poles on each side of their edges as if I were on a swinging platform. After jumping and dancing excitedly, my body jerked, so I looked down. One foot was on top of a *jakdu* blade, but the other foot had slipped in between the blades.

At that very moment, I heard a voice scolding me inside my head. "You should only perform the *jakdu* ritual with a solemn and grateful heart. Why are you promoting yourself and showing off? Come down immediately!"

A cold shiver ran down my spine. Divine Spirit was disciplining me, reminding me not to forget my humble position and to avoid becoming arrogant. I stepped off from the *jakdu* and humbly bowed, grounding my heart.

The next day, an article was published in the newspaper titled "Kim Keum-Hwa Receives an Individual Award." It was a deeply moving moment. Until then, I had never dared to step into the spotlight, even just at a party with family or friends. I always kept a low profile, quietly retreating and trying not to attract attention. I used to worry anxiously about whether my presence as a *mudang* would inconvenience the hosts or make them look bad for knowing me.

Now, I had nothing to hide wherever I went. Scholars studying folk traditions wanted to see my *gut* performances and even came to learn directly from me. Despite this, my financial situation didn't get much better. I still had to worry about feeding and clothing my large family. And yet, gradually, my heart felt more abundant and at ease. Even in poverty, as people began to recognize and acknowledge me, the hardened pain of sorrow and rejection gradually lifted and dissipated. Forgetting even hunger in the presence of Divine Spirit, I truly became a disciple of Spirit.

TWENTY

An Unexpected Marriage

Still, there were days that I felt sentimental. When I returned home to my small bedroom after spending several days away performing *gut*, or when I got disappointed with the business of the human world, I felt lonely, thinking I was all alone in life.

This often surprises people. "Even you, a great shaman, get lonely?" they ask. But why wouldn't I feel loneliness? *Mudangs* are human, after all.

In the Korean Shamanic tradition, marriage is an important element of human life. An unmarried person is thought to have lived an unfulfilled life and often gets ignored as an ancestor after death. That is why the ghosts of unmarried women are often described as scary and full of *han* in Korean folk culture. But while marriage is considered important, *mudangs* tend to be unmarried or experience failed marriages. Why is that? Is it because *mudangs* are required to experience more suffering and pain in a human lifetime?

Some say that Divine Spirit makes shamans struggle in marriages to cut our ties to the human world. It is said that when *mudangs* are too attached to the human world, we become less diligent in serving Spirits and following their guidance. It is even rumored that our gods are jealous of the love and affection we experience with other humans, like our disciples and families.

But I think differently. Our Shamanic gods cherish and love us, the disciples of Divine Spirit. They want us to live happy and joyful lives and want to help us get there. One does not become unhappy simply by becoming a *mudang*. Rather, I believe those already struggling in the human world—unhappy, wounded, not fitting in—end up on the *mudang's* path. Perhaps that is when one's relationships become challenging.

I have been married twice, and both ended in failure. I was hesitant to share this story that I am not proud of, but this part is also a chapter in my life. Although I am not proud of it, I choose not to be ashamed either.

I was twenty-five years old when I met the man who became my second husband. I was very close friends with a couple who had a son named Han-gu, so everyone who knew them called them "Han-gu's Mom" and "Han-gu's Dad." I became a close friend of Han-gu's Mom, sharing secrets and personal stories. I spent many days at their house when I wasn't busy with my Shamanic work.

One day, as I often did, I went over to Han-gu's. In the front yard was a young man, around twenty-seven or twenty-eight years old, talking to Han-gu's Dad. They seemed quite close. His thin face was shadowed and seemed full of worries. Later, I found out his story was quite sad. After only six months of marriage, he was at fault in a serious traffic accident and went to prison. After serving his years-long sentence, he was released, but his wife passed away while he was incarcerated. A baby boy had been born while he was in prison but had been given up to another family as well. Although he did have the basic skills to support himself and tried to start a few businesses, like sign-making and running a retail shop, none worked out. For the last three years, he had gone from one friend's house to another, getting free room and board, and he had just reached Han-gu's.

His name was Kim Myung-Soo. He had heard my life story from Han-gu's Mom, so we became friendly enough. One day, I visited Han-gu's, and he was there sighing, looking grim.

"Mr. Kim, is everything all right? You seem sad."

"That's just how I seem every day, a life of a good-for-nothing," he replied pitifully.

Han-gu's Dad, sitting next to him, snapped at Kim Myung-Soo. "How pathetic do you have to be? A grown man who can't procure his own meals, jumping from one house to another, begging for room and board! I am telling you, today's the last day!"

Han-gu's Dad stormed out, muttering, "The old Korean saying that you save someone from drowning and they complain about lost luggage is so true. How ungrateful!"

I felt bad that Mr. Kim experienced such embarrassment in front of me, so I said, "Oh dear, I don't know what's going on, but it's a bit too harsh."

I said it hoping to be helpful to Mr. Kim, but I could also understand Han-gu's Dad. He sold fish at the dock, yelling all day until his voice went hoarse to feed his family of four, so they didn't have much to share. A friend crashing at their home for a few months, with free room and board, was definitely a burden.

I felt bad for him, so we started having small conversations. His hometown was also in the North, in Sinuiju. At just seventeen years old, he lost his entire family during the Sinuiju Student Revolt.[92]

"I have suffered more than anyone on the entire Korean peninsula," he sighed, sitting in the courtyard and looking at the mountains. He sat there for a long time without realizing how time was passing. His eyes were full of tears.

One day, Han-gu's Mom showed up at my house holding a bundle of rice.

"Keum-Hwa, please bring this rice to my house. Say it is from you, that you brought the rice to feed Kim. Be sure to bring it when my husband is at home and can see you, okay?"

The wife must have felt pity for Kim, even though she, too, was unhappy with her husband's freeloading friend. She thought her husband would feel less bitter and angry if she asked me to pretend to help with the rice. I brought the rice to their house as I was told. Receiving the bundle of rice from my hands, Han-gu's Dad asked in a loud voice, "Oh my, what is the rice for?"

"I brought some rice that you can use for Mr. Kim's meals."

I answered as I was told, but my lying was awkward. Yet Han-gu's Dad was so happy.

"*Aigo*, you are the best."

Kim stood next to Han-gu's Dad, looking sorry. After that, whenever I saw him, I greeted him by asking, "Did you eat today?" If I had any cash on hand, I would sometimes give it to him. It wasn't much, but I hoped it would help feed him.

Honestly, my initial feeling toward him was pity. How sad

---

92. An anti-communist, anti-Soviet revolt led by students of six middle schools on November 23, 1945. It was violently suppressed by the Soviet military, causing many deaths, injuries, and arrests. It led to more demonstrations by the citizens of Sinuiju. Hundreds were killed, thousands were injured, and many of the student leaders arrested were sentenced to Siberia.

that a grown man couldn't earn his own living and had to rely on the charity of his friends? How dire was his situation that he kept returning after being treated shamefully and disrespectfully? It was pitiful to watch; at first, I only felt pity and sympathy for Kim. Eventually, my feelings began to change. I began to wonder what he thought of me and what he thought of my unordinary life.

One day, I casually asked Han-gu's Mom what Kim thought of my being a *mudang.*

"Nothing much," she answered as if it were no big deal. "He said, 'There is no such thing as being noble or common in jobs.'"

By then, Kim and I were seeing each other almost every day. His life was difficult and stunted, and my life was lonely. His desire for comfort and my desire for human warmth naturally pulled us toward each other. Finally, he mentioned marriage.

"Keum-Hwa, I love you with all my heart. Will you marry me?"

It is not every day a woman is proposed to, but I couldn't simply feel happy to receive a marriage proposal. At twenty-five, I was becoming more and more powerful as a spirited shaman, and I had a deep desire to continue growing as a disciple of Divine Spirit rather than settle down into marriage. Also, I couldn't stop thinking that my job as a *manshin* would become a problem in our future life together, even if Kim thought it was no problem then. I was not too concerned about his inability to support me financially, but I was concerned about him regretting his decision someday.

I said no. I thought this was true love, putting his life and happiness before my own.

Although I had declined his proposal, my love for Kim grew deeper. He kept begging me to marry him each time we saw each other. I started to reconsider.

I thought: *He is such a sad and lonely person with no place to go. If I tried my best to support him, couldn't we still become happy together? Two lonely souls coming together in this big world may be enough to live happily ever after...*

There was a thread of hope rising up from my heart. Though it began as pity, maybe that pity was grounded in love. Eventually, I went from "absolutely not" to "maybe."

One day, Han-gu's Mom passed me a handwritten note from Kim. He wanted to meet at a Chinese restaurant. He had written: *Please show up*, as if I had ever stood him up in the past. I felt something must be different this time and was nervous about our promised meeting.

When I entered the Chinese restaurant, he greeted me happily, wearing a nice suit that had clearly been borrowed.

"Keum-Hwa, I beg you sincerely. Please marry me. I want to start a happy family together."

My heart hammered. "I have told you many times already I am not an ordinary woman appropriate for you to seek as a marriage partner," I replied. "That woman is probably somewhere else. My path is already elsewhere."

Once I spoke, tears exploded from my eyes. Why was I born with a fate that prevented me from an ordinary woman's path? The difficult path that was given to me was one upon which I had to see the things ordinary people could not see, acting as the messenger for others from the spirits. Who would understand this path and supportively walk next to me? I shook my head. I had no confidence to navigate and be controlled by the complex human world while tied to one man. I wanted the quiet path, dedicating my whole life to Divine Spirit. My heart was so torn with emotions that I could not stop crying. He held on to my wrist with a firm grip.

"Why must you live like that?" Kim asked. "Please promise to marry me. As you know, I am all alone in this sad world. You have cared for me and helped me, the pitiful, pathetic, and lonely man that I am. I have found the will to live, thanks to you. I think about you day and night. If I could marry you and live with you, I would be the happiest I've ever been."

He started sniffling and crying. I didn't know what to do. We both sat there and cried for a while, our heads down. Then he made a move so sudden I looked up. He had bitten his pinky finger so hard he was bleeding. I was shocked and didn't know what to do.

"What are you doing?"

"I must prove to you how true my heart is since you don't seem to believe what I say. I am making a blood oath that I will never hurt you or make you cry; I will make you happy if you marry me. Can't you believe me now?"

He kept swearing and promising. It was such an intense meeting I felt ungrounded for days afterward. I was so shaken. Han-gu's Mom tried to reunite us, playing the mail carrier by delivering handwritten notes from Kim to me. My heart felt warm whenever I received those love notes.

One day, I received a handwritten invitation to a nearby park. It was raining heavily that day. When Kim saw me approach, he walked up and pulled me into an embrace.

"You've made a mark on my heart ever since we met for the first time. I don't care whether you are a *mudang*. I don't care if you think you are not good enough," he said. "I have received so much love from you in the brief time I have known you. I will never find any other woman who makes me as happy as you. Let's get married."

The park was quiet except for the hard rain. It felt as though I had no more excuses to refuse him. For a long time, whenever I considered marrying Kim, I sensed an ominous feeling that was hard to describe. But I decided to ignore it. I wanted to believe everything he had told me was true. If his heart was sincere and his words true, I would live a simple, peaceful life next to his.

Soon after the marriage, we moved in together. Kim had moved into our home a few days before me, and when I got there, he had already cleaned up and tried to decorate with photos we had taken together and some silk flowers. I liked his effort in trying to decorate to welcome me into our newlywed home. He kept asking me if I liked the flowers, like an excited little boy.

That's how our married life started. Being on each other's side gave us the confidence to face the world and live. It was a short while, but I did experience the joy of an ordinary wife's life of picking out her husband's clothes and setting the dinner table.

TWENTY-ONE

Love, a Path that was Never Meant for Me

Many people had opinions about our marriage. His friends would say, "Why would you want to marry a *manshin*?" But each time, Kim defended me.

"Did you ever feed me one nice meal when I was hungry and freezing?" he told his friends. "Those who speak poorly of my wife are not my true friends and can disappear from my life."

My own family didn't like him either.

"Apparently, such an educated and smart man can't feed himself, have a job, or even remarry for three years after his wife died?" they said. "He is grabbing onto you as if grasping at a straw while drowning because he has no skills or means to live on his own. Give him up."

Nobody wished us well. Only doubtful eyes watched us together. I started to think the only way to quiet the naysayers was to thrive and be happy together. In order to do that, Kim needed to find a steady job.

He had learned to drive while in the military but did not have a license. Back then, you had to go to school for a month and pay a pretty expensive fee to learn to drive. After I had put all my savings into getting our new home together, we didn't have any money left.

When we first met, his appearance had been quite miserable. His suits were old and mended here and there, and his underwear were in rags. As a man, I thought he needed a clean and neat appearance to feel proud to do anything, so I also got him an entirely new wardrobe of suits, shoes, and undershirts. This left us with no money to pay for driving school.

So to support our life together and to pay the driving school tuition, I performed *guts*. One was on Youngjoong Island. I had struggled to find money to pay for the supplies for the ritual. When I finally made enough money, my husband got his driver's license. We felt so accomplished and happy.

There was a family whose elderly mother had been cured by my *gut* after being ill for seven years. Her son was working at the American army base then, and when his mother was completely healed, he bowed respectfully to me and asked how he could repay me. I asked him to find my husband a job. Then I would come to their household and help with housework to show my gratitude. At the time, I was not a famous *manshin* as I am now, but I was still well known as a wise *mudang* who performed powerful *guts*. But I put any pride aside and did even lowly work to find my husband a job.

Finally, he got hired at the US army base. On his first payday, he brought home an envelope with his entire pay and made an offering to the gods with a glass of wine. He held my hands and thanked me.

"I know you worked so hard to get me here. Now our life will be more secure." He became emotional. "You shouldn't continue the work you are doing now. It is too difficult for your body. You must think of your health."

I was touched. Until then, I had to be responsible for my own life, make my own money, and had nobody to discuss with when I had difficulties. Now, I had someone who could support me. My heart felt peaceful, thinking my happiness must be that of a woman loved by a man. The money he made wasn't much, but it was more precious to me than any considerable sum.

He seemed to be making honest efforts for about three months after his hire, although his pay was so meager that I had to make more money to support us.

But as time went by, he started returning home later and later. At first, he said he needed to spend time with his coworkers and came home a couple of hours late. Then he began returning home close to midnight. Sometimes, people would come to see me to settle the bar tabs he owed. Such incidents happened more and more frequently.

Returning home late soon led to Kim not coming home at all. I began catching him in more lies. He had saved a considerable sum of money without telling me and given it to a woman who worked at the bar he frequented. He kept denying it, but I was heartbroken.

Still, I didn't want to push our marriage to the breaking point. I saw my husband as a person with a human heart, thinking he would change his behavior if I approached him with a sincere heart. But his heart seemed unwilling to return to me.

Then I heard from a neighbor that my husband had been seen with another woman as well. Eventually, Kim stopped hiding it altogether, even notifying me when he went to see the other woman. He would open his hand, asking me for money to spend with her, and I would silently hand over cash. He bought multiple shirts, neckties, shoes, and sunglasses and focused on his looks.

I spent many nights worrying alone, waiting, and looking for him everywhere like a crazed woman when he didn't return. I started having headaches, indigestion, and frequent heart palpitations—illnesses caused by stress and repressed anger. One day, I woke up in the morning and started screaming as soon as I opened my eyes. I screamed and screamed, my body thrashing. I felt like I would die from hyperventilating. My husband became angry at me and hit the window with his bare hand, cutting it bloody.

After that, he stopped coming home almost entirely, not returning home for days at a time. When he was home, he never approached me. If our bodies came close enough to touch, he would move away. I got exhausted from waiting, and my eyes were always puffy from crying. Finally, he asked me for a divorce.

"My heart will never return to you," he said. "Living like this is creating suffering for both of us. Breaking up now is an act of care for both of us. If you truly love me, please let me go. You can also start a new path."

I couldn't believe my eyes and ears. *Was this the same man who used to desire me with all his heart? The same man who bit his finger bloody, swearing his love to me? Who made all the sweet promises for our future?*

I did not want a divorce. I enjoyed the protection of a family. But there was no way to hold on to someone whose heart had left. His repeated affairs had hardened my heart. One day, I had enough. I had promised myself I'd never agree to it, but finally, I conceded to a divorce.

At the courthouse, I felt dizzy and faint when signing the paperwork, still hoping to escape the moment. I stood there sweating, then signed the papers as the clerk instructed. It was done. I didn't know where to go as we left the courthouse.

How was I supposed to live now? Who can I ever trust again…?

Once the divorce was finalized, we had our last lunch together at a Chinese restaurant. It was at a Chinese restaurant that I received his passionate proposal and at a Chinese restaurant where we said a tearful farewell. Eleven years of marriage ended. I was twenty-five when I met him and had now become a middle-aged woman.

TWENTY-TWO

Let's Follow Divine Spirit

For a long while, I went almost crazy with heartbreak. After Kim left, I lived in a nightmare of wanting to die. I wrote my will, hid it among my folded clothes, and thought about killing myself every day. A good cry would ease my heart a bit, but then I would be so exhausted after crying that I had no energy to even walk around. When I got tired of crying, I would go touch the desk he used to use and other little things he left behind. I even tried smoking cigarettes. No matter what I did, I couldn't put my heart back together.

One day, a friend came by to visit me. She saw me suffering and, frustrated, said, "If you are going to live like this, it's better to die after all. I thought you were a smart woman, but you are a fool. A few days ago, I saw Kim, and he was dressed up sharply, walking around happy and well, while your mother said you even ran out of rice in the pantry. Why die? Get revenge!"

When she said *revenge*, my ears perked. *How could I make him regret leaving me?*

But soon, I shook my head.

I must pray to Spirit. If I were abandoned because I am a mudang, all I have is Spirit. If I pray to my gods sincerely, they will help.

That evening, at midnight, I went out to the backyard and prayed under the moon with an offering of clear water.

"Divine Spirit, your disciple Kim Keum-Hwa is now only thirty-six years old. Please show me the way. When I became a *mudang* many years ago, my spirit mother gave me *gongsu* that if I were to climb high mountains and walk the lonely path, there would be a place for me to stand. How much longer must I walk the lonely path, and where is the place for me to stand?"

After twenty-one days of such early morning prayer, I heard the sound of wind blowing at my ear and a voice.

"Go to Seoul. To Seoul."

I bowed and turned towards the direction I heard the voice coming from. Of course, there was no one.

Seoul? I thought. *I don't know anyone there ... But if Spirit told me to go to Seoul, there must be a reason. I will rely on Divine Spirit and go to Seoul.*

I immediately sold my house in Bupyeong and moved to Seoul near Noryangjin. It was 1966.

Many years later, a journalist interviewing me asked about my marriage.

"He cheated on you and abandoned you. Why did you try so hard not to get a divorce?"

"You can call me old-fashioned, but I felt that a husband was protection for a woman," I explained. "I thought a woman without a husband was like an empty courtyard without a fence: unprotected. In this harsh world, too many shameful eyes want to come inside the courtyard that stays open and unprotected. I was afraid of losing that protection."

Still, when I considered people who were not as kind or greedier than me, all living happily with their own families, I wondered why I couldn't have even one partner to share my heart with. Sometimes, I became sad comparing other people's lives to my lonely situation. But I braced my heart and wiped my tears. If I became so weak and dwelled in self-pity over such small matters, how could people rely on me to help with their suffering?

A *mudang* is a person who must embrace all the *han* and tears of others. Because I have been deeply hurt and suffered in this human life, I can understand others' pain and heal their suffering. One should be so grateful to be blessed to live a happy life. Even the pain and difficulties of life can offer lessons and wisdom. I want to encourage everyone to feel gratitude for both happiness and unhappiness.

Kim Keum-Hwa at home with her mother doing laundry, circa 1973.

A photo during a *Daedong-gut* circa 1987. Kim Keum-Hwa returned to the ritual site while dancing, after greeting and receiving spirits at the mountain.

Right page: Kim Keum-Hwa during a *Mansudaetak-gut*, circa 1980.
Next page: Kim Keum-Hwa at thirty-four years old with a friend. At the time, it was a photo trend to dress women up as gentlemen.

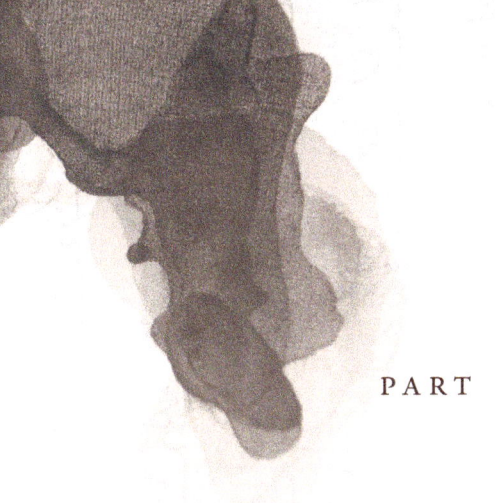

PART 3

Let Us Share Blessings and Release the Bitterness of Han

The *gut* is at once a spirited celebration and a tearful catharsis. Those who have never witnessed a *gut* call it fearful, but that is because they do not understand it.

by Kim Keum-Hwa

TWENTY-THREE

The *Gut* That Moved Americans

If I were to identify one of the happiest moments of my life, it was when I participated in the 100th-anniversary commemorative performance of the US–Korea Diplomatic Relations held in the United States in 1982. While I have performed countless times abroad since then, none of those performances have left as many memories as that event—my first-ever performance outside Korea.

It all began one day in 1981 when I received a phone call.

"Will you come to the United States next year for the 100th-anniversary commemorative performance of US–Korea Diplomatic Relations?"

The person who called me was Dr. Zo Zayong. The late Dr. Zo was a graduate of Harvard's Architecture program and had a deep and abiding interest in Korean folklore. He also founded the Emile Museum[93] and served as its director.

Hearing those words, my mind went blank, and I forgot to speak, merely holding the receiver in my hand. The 100th-anniversary commemorative event was of national importance, and to be invited to such a grand event left me overwhelmed to the point where I couldn't distinguish between dream and reality.

"Of course, I will go," I finally replied. "Thank you for inviting me to such a significant event. It's an honor."

The performance was scheduled for May 1982. I was so excited that I even lost sleep for several days after the call. However, a few days later, Dr. Zo Zayong called me again, sounding worried. He told me that the chairman of the event's organizing committee was furious upon hearing about the inclusion of "*mudang gut*" in the program. The chairman deemed it a national disgrace to showcase a Shamanic ceremony at the 100th-anniversary commemorative performance and ordered its immediate removal. Despite this, Dr. Zo, who had a keen interest in folk culture, was determined to find a way to include the ritual performance in the program. Not only was Dr. Zo personally invested, but the director of the Smithsonian Institution, who had watched my *gut* performance on KBS, also specifically requested my invitation.

"Is there another term or expression we can use instead of *mudang gut*?" he asked.

---

93. 에밀레 박물관, Zo Zayong founded Emile Museum/Gallery in 1968, named after the Emile Bell from the ancient Silla kingdom, displaying his private collection of Korea's traditional arts like *minhwa* (민화, folk paintings), arts and artifacts of Korean Shamanism and Samshin philosophy, and other folklore artifacts. It thrived for many years before getting shutdown after his death in 2001. In 2022, it re-opened as a mixed-use cultural event space thanks to the efforts by Zo Zayong Folk Culture Research Foundation. It is located in Boeun, Chungcheong province.

"I'm not sure. A *mudang gut* is a *mudang gut*. What other name can it be called?" I replied. "In my hometown, we call it *Cheolmuri-gut*. If we have to change it, maybe we can call it the '*Cheolmuri* Dance'? But if they are so opposed to it, would changing the name really make any difference?"

But Dr. Zo was delighted by the suggestion of the *Cheolmuri* Dance, saying, "Oh, that's great. Let's go with that."

Then Dr. Zo said he would contact me again and ended the call. I was disappointed, wondering if I had gotten my hopes up for nothing. But after a few days, Dr. Zo called me once more.

"It's done! You will participate in the program under the name *Cheolmuri* Dance."

Once my participation was confirmed, I felt much calmer. It made me realize that I had agonized and worried needlessly, as whether I could participate or not was entirely up to the will of Spirit. In May of the following year, 1982, I boarded a plane to Los Angeles. On the dawn of my departure to the United States, I went to my shrine with a purified and resolute heart and clasped my hands together in prayer.

"Thank you, Divine Spirit of Heaven and Earth. I express my gratitude for choosing someone as inadequate as me to be a *mudang* and represent my country as far away as the United States. Our *gut* tradition will now become known and acknowledged by even more people. Please watch over me so that I may safely return after completing the performance."

In the end, the *Yangju* Mask Dance, *Sinawi*,[94] and our *Cheolmuri* Dance groups were selected as the representatives for the event. We began with an invited performance in Los Angeles.

---

94. 시나위, also called *Shimbang gok* (심방곡) as in "shaman's song", folk music driving from the ancient Silla Kingdom with a distinct vocal and instrumental exchange style often used in Shamanic rituals in Korea.

After spending a few days conducting brief *gut* performances at locations such as Los Angeles Korean Park and the Los Angeles Museum, we were ready to head to the main event at Knoxville's World's Fair Park.

When we arrived at Knoxville Airport, the organizers were there to greet us. However, their gaze toward us was critical and disapproving. One of them took Dr. Zo aside and appeared to say something unpleasant. While Dr. Zo did not say much, I couldn't help but worry. It appeared that the event organizers were not welcoming and seemed hostile. I was concerned that we had come all this way only to be unable to perform and would return to Korea without having served any purpose.

Our group got into the cars provided by the event organizers, and we were taken to a secluded motel. They briefly informed us that a bus would be sent at the scheduled time for the performance and then left abruptly. It was already evening, and everyone was ravenous since we hadn't had a proper meal on the plane. We tried to find a suitable restaurant with our guide, but lacking the means, we ended up having a meager dinner of just a few pieces of bread.

The next morning, a few people went to the city to purchase rice, pickled cucumbers, potatoes, and zucchini to prepare a real meal. Strangely enough, no matter how much soy sauce we added to our stew, it tasted bitter instead of savory. Some said that perhaps American soy sauce tastes different, so they continued pouring more of it. When I tasted the soy sauce, I realized it was actually Coke. It turned out that they had mistakenly bought a large plastic bottle of Coke—which we had never seen in Korea at that time—thinking it was soy sauce. We all laughed until our bellies ached.

It rained heavily on the day of the performance. We went down to the motel lobby earlier than the appointed time to wait for the bus arranged by the organizers. However, even after the scheduled time had passed, the bus still hadn't arrived.

"What's going on? We're going to be late."

Frantically running back and forth, Dr. Zo went out to the main road and flagged down a van. After explaining our predicament, we got a ride in that vehicle.

"Those bastards!" he exclaimed.

Dr. Zo finally explained what had happened at the airport a few days prior. The organizers had been displeased with our shabby appearance. They had berated him for the absurdity of putting such scruffy-looking people on stage for such a grand international celebration. In our case, this was the first overseas trip for all of us, and we were not wealthy enough to dress up in fancy attire. Dr. Zo said he had politely persuaded them, but it seemed like they deliberately did not send the car, which made him angry. It was pouring rain, and the performances had already begun by the time we departed the motel.

I suppressed my sorrowful and angry feelings and prayed to Divine Spirit that everything would go well. The people I had traveled with were all modest and kind-hearted individuals. Notably, the *Yangju* Mask Dance group consisted of many elderly people. They had gladly joined this journey, dragging their old and weary bodies across the world, inspired by the idea that they were representing Korea and bringing pride to their country. I fervently prayed for all of us to safely complete our performances and return home with joyful hearts.

When we arrived at the performance venue, a dancer from the National Dance Company of Korea was concluding a court dance and transitioning into a creative *gut*, where she created a *suwangpo*,[95] a path to the afterlife, with a cotton cloth. I was momentarily stupefied. From her extravagant attire to the brilliant makeup and adornments, she was dazzling to the point of being blinding. As I looked around at our group, we appeared like rural dwellers visiting the city for the first time—a ragged and pitiable sight. We all stood awkwardly next to the performance stage; our spirits withered.

Suddenly, an individual from the Korean consulate approached us and began yelling angrily, "How can you show up this late! You're too late, and there's no way we can have you perform. It's impossible."

Dr. Zo attempted to explain our situation, but the man didn't even try to listen. Instead, he kicked us all out. Our entire group was forced away from the venue. Mr. Zo became so enraged that his face turned red, and he stormed back inside.

"No, this cannot be."

Muttering to himself, Dr. Zo turned to us and said, "There is no way we're just going to turn back. Everyone, please gather your strength and follow me."

Dr. Zo led us toward the alley of the building. We followed him into what looked like a shabby office, where we unloaded our supplies and changed our clothes. At that moment, we were all of one heart.

"Now, we must all be united in one mind," he said. "If we scatter, we die; if we unite, we survive. Let's each quickly prepare ourselves and give our best."

All of our eyes were sparkling with determination. Dr. Zo

---

95. 수왕포, a fabric bridge made of white cotton cloth during a Shamanic ritual to represent the sacred bridge connecting the human world and the spirit world. The cloth bridge is spilt during the *gut* to ensure the departed crosses over peacefully to the afterlife.

encouraged us all, saying we had come too far to give up now, urging us to gather courage and give all we had. On one side, I prepared an altar with rice cakes steamed from rice flour, fruit, alcohol, and other items. Meanwhile, the performers of the *Sinawi* changed their attire and went upstage to perform. However, the stage was already darkened, and the carpet was being rolled up. We were all taken aback and became flustered. At that moment, Dr. Zo strode forward onto the stage. In fluent English, he began speaking to the audience.

"Ladies and gentlemen, our performance today is not yet over. The carpet is being rolled up because the following performances cannot be done on it. Please take a seat as the show is about to begin. The next performances are very special, showcasing the beauty of Korean folk traditions. Please do not miss this wonderful opportunity!"

Despite Dr. Zo's words, the audience remained standing and did not sit back down. The *Yangju* group got on stage and began their mask dance. However, the audience began leaving the performance venue one by one. The *Sinawi* and *Yangju* Mask dancers performed for fifteen minutes, unable to capture their audience's attention. In an instant, fear and uncertainty overwhelmed me. Tears welled up as I feared I would be kicked off the stage, unable to perform even a single passage of the *gut* when I was so close to this opportunity.

Just then, Dr. Zo raised his voice and introduced our *gut* performance.

"The people I want to introduce now are representative shamans of Korea. With great difficulty, we have managed to present you with these individuals who dwell in the most mystical and numinous realms. Let us all have a festive ritual with the Knoxville Mountain God and the gods brought over by these esteemed shamans. Let's dance together, sing songs, share the prepared foods, and receive the blessings that will come into your homes. Now, please enjoy this extraordinary *gut* ceremony!"

Dr. Zo, who had moved towards the stage exit, hastily gestured to me on the opposite side. It was a signal for me to quickly enter the stage. I layered on all the attire for each of the *gut* passages at once. I held the *ilweoldae*—the sun and moon staff—in my right hand, and in my left hand, I held a fan and bell rattle. On my head, I wore a *hosugat*[96] and a flower *gat*.

"We welcome, we greet Ilweolseongshin.
We welcome and greet Cheonji-shinmyeong.[97]
Here comes Hwangung Cheonwang, Grandfather Dangun,
the Seven Star God is descending.
We welcome and greet Knoxville Mountain God.
We have come from the East, where the sun rises."

My legs trembled uncontrollably as I danced and sang at the top of my voice. Although I knew I hadn't been possessed by Divine Spirit, my whole body trembled and shook as if I had. Goosebumps ran down my arms and legs. There was only one thought in my mind: *How can I stop the audience from leaving and bring this* gut *to the finish?*

If I were to fail at this performance and return home defeated, I knew that this experience would become a lingering sorrow and pain in my heart. I yearned to invite others into a magnificent and moving feast between the spirits and humans.

---

96. 호수갓, a hat worn by *mudang*s in the Hwanghae Province, adorned with the feathers of white herons and tiger beards.

97. 천지신명, the Divine Spirit of Heaven and Earth, a deity that presides over the harmony of heaven and earth.

As I stood in the center of the stage, suppressing the trembling in my heart, I bit my lip and encouraged myself: *Let's do this. Raise your strength!*

I leaped high on the stage, and at that moment, a strong divine energy surged from the tips of my toes. At once, I reached a state of complete ecstasy, unable to distinguish whether my feet touched the ground or if I floated upon the air. As sweat poured from me like rain, I realized I couldn't discern whether any audience members were present. Still, I leaped and bounded across the stage, traversing its expanse until I finally landed on the wooden platform where the *jakdu* blades were positioned. Without hesitating, I jumped at once onto the *jakdu* blades. I danced on the *jakdu* for quite a while.

However, inevitably, one must descend from the blades. There comes a time when even the divine energy that soars and surges toward the sky must return to Earth. I closed my eyes and stood still, surrounded by a hauntingly silent audience. I felt my strength draining like I was on the verge of collapse.

It didn't go well, I thought. *But I know I gave it my all. If this is the will of Divine Spirit, I must accept it gracefully.*

I slowly opened my eyes to an unbelievable sight. The people who had previously left the auditorium had returned, and the hall was tightly packed. Suddenly, an overwhelming chorus of applause and shouts erupted from the nearly 6,000-seat audience, including those who had watched the performance from the extended outdoor seating. Even in the areas where the stage lights did not reach, I could make out people clapping. At once, I started pulling the audience members onto the stage. Everyone joined in, wearing the attire I had handed out, and we danced together. It was a joyous culmination of a *gut* in which stray ghosts are released with food and dance. The stage was filled with people of all colors, creating a vibrant scene, while below the stage, television cameras from various broadcasting networks busily captured the moment. A big white man, who had been dancing passionately, lifted me onto his back as we continued to dance across the stage.

Ah, thank you, Divine Spirit! Thank you, Grandfather spirit, for granting my wish and watching over me. Thank you!

I wept with gratitude to Divine Spirit. Holding an armful of *gut* offerings, I shared bites of the food with the audience. They savored the Korean greens and rice cakes, and each person offered one or two dollars in return. As the performance concluded triumphantly, the demeanor the event organizers showed toward us underwent a noticeable change.

"We are sincerely sorry. We were ignorant and made a lot of mistakes," one said. "Please extend your generosity in forgiveness and let go of any lingering resentment."

The person in charge bowed repeatedly, expressing his apology. They insisted on taking us out to a restaurant in rented cars instead of returning us straight to our lodgings. It seemed the organizers had completely transformed after the performance. Dr. Zo, who feigned indifference, smiled and winked at me when our eyes met. I conveyed my gratitude to Dr. Zo for persevering until the very end and making this performance a reality.

After that day, we continued performing in Knoxville for twenty-five days. Then we traveled to Washington D.C., New Jersey, New York, and other places, concluding a successful series of performances that spanned about three months. A museum in D.C. took great care to film our *gut* for documentary footage.

I still take pride in the *gut* I performed that day. I believe that how everything unfolded truly forged the essence of a genuine cultural relationship between Korea and America. Despite the language barrier, we could read each other's hearts through the warm gazes of the people filling the stage. I could sense their sincere welcome and efforts to understand and embrace the practice of *gut*, with which they were unfamiliar. Through the ceremony, people living in different parts of the Earth, with different languages and skin colors, connected and became one—to me, that is the true meaning of "communication" and "bonding."

TWENTY-FOUR

An Encounter Between Native American and Korean Gods

So our planned two-week performance in the United States had extended into a three-month tour, taking us to various cities. Being in a completely foreign country, one of the most heartwarming and joyful experiences was encountering fellow Koreans and indulging in Korean food. The members of the Korean-American community were very kind and would often prepare meals, inviting us to join them. Among the Korean diaspora living in the U.S., there were many Christians, and often, before a meal, someone would say, "Let's pray." As if they had agreed collectively, everyone would join hands and recite the Lord's Prayer, which began with the words, "Our Father, who art in heaven, hallowed by thy name..." I often sat there feeling a bit awkward, but at some point, I started to silently pray along.

"*Hananim*, will you also watch over me as you do for them?" I asked. "Please, in harmony with the deities I serve, *Cheonji-shinmyeong* and *Dangun Grandfather*, please take care of me."

When others closed with "Amen!" I quickly said, "Thank you," and concluded my prayer.

One stop on our U.S. tour included a performance in the state of Connecticut. This state, with its challenging pronunciation, holds many memorable moments. Before starting the performance, while reciting the invocation, I struggled with pronouncing "Connecticut." Instead of "Connecticut," I kept stumbling and said something like "Cot-ju-cock-cock," which turned the venue into a sea of laughter.

For that performance, we were housed in a dormitory at the University of Connecticut, and it was quite a memorable experience to stay in a student dorm at an American university. One evening, as I returned to my fifth-floor room after dinner, I encountered Kim, the *daegeum* flute player, when I got off the elevator. Earlier that evening, he had been involved in a minor argument with other performers, so his face was gloomy. I saw him pacing the hallway, looking fidgety, and returned to my room. After changing my clothes and lying down, I was suddenly startled by a loud, piercing noise. The sound gradually grew louder until it became so loud that it felt like my head was shaking. Startled, I opened the door and stepped out into the hallway, which I found in complete chaos. Even if I couldn't understand the language, I could instantly sense that something urgent was happening.

The hallway was filled with people like me who had fled their rooms in astonishment, others who had hastily covered themselves with towels as if they ran out mid-shower—people of all colors and shapes mixed up in a great commotion. One male student had even rushed out of his room without wearing underwear.

I followed the students down the emergency staircase. Fire trucks were already outside and more were still arriving with sirens blaring. People were gathered in circles, murmuring anxiously and looking up at the dorm. Amidst the chaos, I suddenly remembered that I had left my medicine bundle and passport inside. I tried to go back into the building, but firefighters blocked my way. I helplessly paced back and forth.

The commotion lasted for a long while, but there was no fire. At that point, the firefighters began investigating who had needlessly pulled the fire alarm, needing to identify the specific bell that was pulled in order to turn off the alarms. The alarm continued blaring, leading to the arrival of more than twenty fire trucks. I don't know what came over him, but Kim, the *daegum* player, pointed at me and claimed to have seen me press something on the fifth floor. People rushed towards me, causing chaos and confusion.

"Shaman Kim, why did you go around touching things when you don't know anything about them?" someone said.

"With all these fire trucks here, you will surely be fined. Selling your house won't begin to cut it," said another.

"They will surely file a claim for damages against the Korean government," someone even threatened.

I felt like I'd been struck by lightning while sleeping. People pointed their fingers at me and didn't even give me a chance to defend myself. Aside from my worries about a fine, I was hurt and ashamed that such a disgraceful incident happened abroad. Since I don't speak English, I couldn't explain myself clearly. While the Koreans argued among themselves, a foreigner came over and pointed at Kim, claiming to have seen him touching something near the fire alarm on the fifth floor.

Perhaps he pressed the emergency bell instead of the elevator button and blamed me for some unfathomable reason, leaving me to deal with his predicament. Although I was relieved to have been cleared of the misunderstanding, I still felt embarrassed by the actions of my companions. From then on, until I left the dormitory, I kept my distance from the fire alarm. I also stood far away from any buttons, fearing that I might accidentally press the wrong one. People continued to speculate about possible fines and the need for promissory notes. However, after that night, there was no further mention of the fire alarm incident.

Instead, the day we left the city, the mayor arrived and personally awarded us all "honorary citizenship." They even arranged a bus for us to travel to our next performance venue. We were grateful and humbled by such generous hospitality.

We were welcomed everywhere we went. During our *gut* performance at the Smithsonian, we had the pleasure of meeting the museum director and his wife, who were avid fans of the tradition of *gut*. Every time I performed a *gut*, they passionately danced along, matching my own Divine-fueled energy. The director even said it felt like the spirits had descended upon his wife.

At the outdoor performances in front of the National Assembly, several Native Americans would come to watch our *gut* rituals every day. Their interest in our *gut* was genuine and joyful. Whenever I offered them rice cakes for blessings, they would place a dollar on the offering plate or adorn my wrist with crystal beaded bracelets. They also presented me with gifts of small perfumes. During the finale of the *gut*, when we all danced together, they leaped and danced with a vigor that seemed as if it would send them soaring into the sky.

One day, they asked me to meet them separately. When the Native Americans saw me, they gave a momentary look of surprise. According to the interpreter, they had seen a five-colored light emitting around me. They, too, were individuals with extraordinary energy.

On another day, we were invited into their home. When we arrived, we discovered they also had a sacred altar inside their house. Their carefully arranged shrine was adorned with photographs of their ancestors, and ceremonial bowls and plates filled with water and food. After sharing a meal, they filled our glasses, played musical instruments, and danced along. It was a spirited dance in which they shook their bodies fiercely while pounding the ground with their palms. I was astonished when they placed a dollar bill on my forehead as we danced. It reminded me of the same customs in Korea. I prostrated myself before their sacred shrine and offered my blessings.

> "Manshin Kim Keum-Hwa bows down before you on American soil.
> Despite differences in our languages and cultures, I trust that Spirit is one.
> May the gods who watch over Korea and America bring harmony
> and ensure the safety and peace of our nations.
> May Korea be free of external threats
> and may our split country torn in two be reunited in peace and oneness.
> May the gods bless the generous people of Korea and grant us prosperity.
> Here, kneeling and offering this prayer in sincerity,
> I ask for your blessings and success as we return to Korea."

We embraced one another and exchanged more blessings. Although we worshipped different gods, an unknown force had called us here and united us in a deep spiritual embrace. Beyond our differences in religion and race, there was a profound encounter between the American folk gods and my own gods.

On the day I left the United States, I looked down from the

plane during take-off and had many thoughts. I had witnessed a lot in America, and I couldn't help but feel envious of the lively children playing on the vast and free land and the elderly savoring a blissful existence in their old age. Observing their beaming smiles, mutual concessions, and acts of kindness, I pondered the meaning of living a worthy life. I truly envied those who resided in a prosperous nation where they could wholeheartedly pursue their lives without being constrained by the opinions of others. Furthermore, while *guts* were often dismissed and scorned as "superstition" in my homeland, they were embraced with endless fascination and appreciation by the people here. The sincere efforts of the Americans I met to respect and comprehend a culture entirely different from theirs resonated with a deep sense of cultural generosity.

My Korean ancestors lived on a small piece of land, constantly facing foreign invasions, and thus had always carried the burden of *han*. Even the ground, stained with the blood of our ancestors, has been torn into North and South—so how to even begin untangling the pervasive *han* and grief? I thought that one day, after some years had passed, I would perform a *Hanpuri*[98] *gut* for Korea's ancestors.

Finally, I was back in my neighborhood. My mother, leaning on a cane, came out to the main road to welcome me home.

"My daughter, how courageous and mighty you are!" my mother greeted me. "I have been waiting for you this whole time, ready to carry you home on my back."

My mother seemed so proud that her daughter had traveled to the distant land of the United States to perform the *gut*. I quickly lifted my mother onto my back as she pushed her back toward me. Her frail body felt as light as a bundle of straw. Carried on the back

---

98. 한풀이, the untangling and healing of *han*.

of her beloved daughter, who filled her with pride, my mother was as radiant as a triumphant warrior returning from battle.

"Hey, everyone, come and look here," she called out. "My daughter went all the way to America and gained fame through her *gut* performance. She went all the way across the ocean to represent our country."

My mother was absolutely delighted, resembling a small child beaming with pride. My nose tingled, and I moved one of the hands supporting her to wipe away my tears. As my body swayed slightly, my mother exclaimed, "Hey, don't let me fall off! I'm about to fall off!" and clung tightly to me.

My mother was moved that her daughter, who had endured so much hardship and pain as a *mudang*, had gained recognition in the United States. Not only that, but the successful performances abroad helped me wash away the accumulated sorrows and bitterness in my heart.

Divine Spirit had granted me this precious opportunity to venture into the larger world and learn. Perhaps they sought to inspire me to expand my perspective and embrace and nurture even more people.

TWENTY-FIVE

Recovering a Grandfather's Remains Through Dream

In the spring of 1972, I went to my favorite flower shop in Seoul to read fortunes for several people. Among them was a young newlywed whose future appeared exceptionally ominous. The reading indicated that something unfortunate might occur to the patriarch of her family towards the end of June or early July. Although I sensed that he might pass away, I couldn't bring myself to tell her outright. Instead, I mentioned a possible misfortune and suggested a *gut*. The newlywed agreed and left after receiving a scheduled date for the ritual. However, just a few days after her reading, she gave me a call.

"Oh, I'm terribly sorry," she said. "When I discussed the *gut* with my husband, he became upset and vehemently refused, claiming it was a waste and beyond our means. I won't be able to proceed with the ritual."

At times like this, I find myself in a predicament, torn between speaking up or staying silent. If I were to share the true reason for performing the *gut*, it could be misconstrued as a threat to force a ritual. Yet if I were to remain silent, I fear I may unwittingly incur the anger of Divine Spirit. Plus, it's someone's life that's on the line. In my early days as a *mudang*, I felt compelled to persuade a potential client or patient to carry out a *gut*. If I happened to have enough food at home, I even offered to perform the ritual for free to ward off potential harm. However, as time went on, it became increasingly difficult to continue trying to persuade those reluctant to hold a *gut*. People often viewed me suspiciously and misunderstood my intent, leaving deep scars in my heart.

But after much deliberation, I decided to cautiously relay the information to the newlywed.

"Listen to me very carefully," I began. "The fortune reading revealed that your father-in-law is likely to pass away. It seems that during the Lunar months of June or July, there is a possibility that he might take his own life via water or railroad. Please be aware and take utmost precautions."

The newlywed seemed eager to just hang up the phone. It was disheartening, considering that someone's life was at stake, but there was nothing more I could do. Instead, I prayed for the grandfather every time I entered the shrine at dawn. Several months passed in this way.

Then, on the day of *Chilseok*, I received a call from the newlywed, who urgently asked if I would come over. Since it was *Chilseok*, my home was bustling with my regular clients who had gathered to express their gratitude. They had brought rice cakes and fruit to celebrate the sacred day with me, making it impossible for me to leave my home. However, I couldn't ignore the situation and visited the flower shop early the next day. Due to a disturbing dream I'd had the night before, I didn't feel entirely refreshed. The flower shop was crowded with the relatives of the newlywed woman. She rushed to me, her face pale, and grasped my hand tightly.

"What to do?" she cried. "My father-in-law left home five days ago and still hasn't returned. What should we do about this?"

The young woman, on the verge of tears, looked at me with a strained face. However, the rest of the family members seemed wary of me. I placed purified water and rice on the divination table and silently closed my eyes.

In my mind, I recited the grandfather's family name, his age, and the fact that he'd left home on the third day of the Lunar July before inquiring about his condition.

As soon as I asked, I heard a reply to my question.

"He went to the Han River and drowned!"

I opened my eyes and stared at the owner of the flower shop, thinking she'd been the one to speak.

How strange. I thought, puzzled. *If they knew the old man drowned in the Han River, they should go and retrieve his body. Why would they ask me to perform divination?*

"Hey, what did you say just now?" I asked the woman. "Did you mention Han River Road?"

The owner of the shop looked at me with a perplexed expression. "I didn't say anything," she replied.

At that moment, I recalled my dream from the night before. The dream, which had been hazy in the morning, suddenly resurfaced with the vivid clarity of a remembered movie scene.

I was standing on an asphalt road in front of a house. Across from me, in the distance, a small pickup truck was approaching. The truck carried four or five people, one of whom was lying down. The vehicle came to a halt in front of me. The person lying in the middle brushed aside the thin blanket, stood up, and walked toward me. I greeted him with an embrace.

"I don't know you, but I entrust my children to you," he said. "Please take good care of them."

After uttering those words, the person released his grip on my hand and walked up the asphalt road. Then he crossed a small bridge and abruptly plunged into the water. Stunned, I shouted, questioning why he was trying to take his own life. The person revealed that he carried deep wounds in his heart and could not bear to live any longer. I looked closely and noticed his round, flat face accentuated by prominent cheekbones. His voice echoed so loudly that it could shake an entire mountain. I followed him down to the bottom of the bridge, but my left foot slipped into the murky water. The man urged me not to follow him and swiftly vanished into the water.

After reliving my dream, I opened my eyes slowly and cast the mound of rice used to perform divination. Then I proceeded to explain my reading.

"If you walk a short distance from your house, there is a shop. Go there first and inquire after your father-in-law," I said. "Then continue following the road in front of the shop. When you reach the riverbank, keep going towards the Han River. There, you will meet a second group of people and have a conversation. You will hear news of your father-in-law from the third person you encounter."

I explained the place her father-in-law might have passed in detail—a vantage point from which the Second Han River Bridge was visible. I couldn't shake off the sight of the houses lined up along the Kimpo riverside. When I asked the newlywed if she knew anyone who lived nearby, she said no.

"In that case, your father-in-law was near the Kimpo riverside just before his death," I told her. "Hurry there, now. You won't be able to find him after 2 o'clock this afternoon."

After hearing my words, the newlywed and her family rushed out. The grandmother, known for harshly scolding her husband when he drank, silently shed endless tears.

Upon returning home, I began to worry that my divination might be wrong and performed another. I fervently prayed to the gods, seeking guidance on whether a *gut* could bring back the grandfather. Strangely enough, the divination table appeared white, as if draped in a white sheet. It was an ominous sign.

I put the divination table away and went into my room to lie down. Even lying down, I couldn't find peace of mind. What if the family couldn't find his body? Had it really been necessary to give such detailed directions and act like I knew everything, potentially causing more problems? Why hadn't I simply indicated the general direction like other shamans would have done? But I had made up my heart. After all, hadn't I decided to follow the guidance of the gods, understanding that defying them would only bring more suffering? Since I had consulted and relied solely on the gods, I decided to release all other thoughts.

Before long, the telephone rang. It was the flower shop.

"*Ajumoni*, are you a ghost or a human?"

These words came tumbling out of the telephone receiver. Finally, I was able to breathe a sigh of relief. My divination had been accurate, and they had found the grandfather. One of the family members explained to me how they found his body.

They went to the shop I had mentioned and asked if the owner had seen the grandfather. The owner informed them that he had stopped by a few days ago to purchase a bottle of alcohol and a pack of cigarettes before walking toward the Han River. The shop owner didn't have any further information. The family members left the shop and made their way to the riverbank.

Looking down from the embankment, they spotted the grandfather's friends sitting under the bridge, drinking. The son went down and inquired if they had any news.

"How would we know anything even his children don't know?" the men angrily retorted.

But when the family looked toward the Second Han River Bridge, they saw a man walking there. They approached him and asked if he had heard of anyone recently dying nearby. The man pointed across the bridge and spoke.

"See that ambulance over there? They came to transport the body after receiving a report."

Startled, the son raced towards the ambulance. His father's body had already been recovered, and people were swarming around it. Due to it being summer and the body having been pulled from the water, it was extensively damaged. It was impossible to confirm whether the remains belonged to his father.

"Has he been identified yet?" the son asked the emergency personnel who had come to investigate, his heart trembling with anxiety. They responded that they did not know and gestured to where the deceased's belongings lay. There the son could make out a pile of white clothes—no doubt the traditional pants and jacket that belonged to his father. Before jumping into the water, his father had carefully removed his outer garments, layer by layer, and even placed his dentures on top, arranging everything neatly. The son sank to the ground beside his father's belongings and wept uncontrollably.

The family then asked me if they could bring the body back home. I replied that those who died outside must be buried outside. Then I hung up the phone.

It felt as if my heart was being ripped apart. As a *mudang*, I couldn't help but believe I should have done something to prevent this calamity, regardless of what others said. I experienced a deep sense of guilt, as if I had allowed the grandfather to die. I also felt ashamed and questioned my qualifications as a *mudang*.

After the funeral ritual, the deceased's son called me. He expressed regret for not following my counsel and wept with deep remorse. His cries only intensified my sorrow. The son pleaded for a meeting, so we arranged to meet at a teahouse. The son and his wife arrived early, waiting for me. Dressed in mourning attire, the son approached me and greeted me politely.

"Thank you for helping us find my father's remains. If I hadn't found my father's body, I would have carried a lifelong burden of *han* and filial impiety."

The son extended a white envelope, explaining that it represented his family's sincerity. Taken aback, I firmly declined, pushing the envelope away.

"I cannot accept this. I was merely following the divine instructions of my gods. I will accept your grateful heart and offer it back to Spirit."

However, he refused to give up, insistent on expressing his gratitude and repeating that I had saved him from a life of filial disgrace. We went back and forth for a while. Then suddenly, I remembered the request from the person in my dream, asking me to take care of his children. The deceased had left behind eight children.

"If you truly wish to give me this money, let's use it for a *Neokgeoji-gut*,[99]" I suggested. "Since your father passed away in the water, it is likely that he couldn't find a peaceful place to rest. Let's console his soul and ensure there will be no future misfortune in your family."

---

99. 넋걷이굿, a ritual to retrieve and appease the soul of those who died in water.

The spirits of those who die suddenly and away from home carry regrets and grudges. Even after death, it is common for a spirit to wander in the world for two to three years before attaching itself to a family member and causing harm. Therefore, I thought it would be a good idea to perform a *Neokgeoji-gut* to prevent any potential damage to the descendants. This time, the son readily agreed to my proposal.

The day we performed the *gut* for the old man, there was a torrential downpour. That year's monsoon season was particularly intense, leaving the surrounding area nearly submerged. We went out onto the Second Han River Bridge towards Kimpo, where the elderly man had passed away, to perform the *gut*. The current was so fierce that a *mudang* might be swept away in the rushing water during the ritual. Generally, when performing this soul retrieval *gut*, the pulling force of the soul could be so powerful that there were times when a *mudang* was dragged into the water. Thus, it is common practice that a cotton rope is tied around the *mudang's* waist, and the people standing outside the water hold firmly onto the rope while the ritual is performed.

On the day of the ritual, I was feeling unwell and weak, so my disciple took over the passage of retrieving the soul. However, as soon as the *gut* began and the shaman entered the water, she immediately fainted. She couldn't overcome the vengeful power of the soul. I was so startled I pulled the cotton rope with all my strength. But, at that moment, my left foot slipped and slid into the river's murky waters. I was stunned because it happened exactly like it had in my dream. My disciple took a while to awaken while I successfully completed the rest of the *gut*. From then on, the grandfather's family members became my long-standing regulars.

The body of the grandfather may have easily never been found. However, through his family's fervent prayers and Great Spirit's benevolence, the body was recovered with divine assistance. When people encounter misfortunes or challenging situations, they often just passively accept it as their destiny and give up. But even when we strive to meet these challenges head-on, there are moments when they surpass our human efforts. In these moments, when we reach the limits of our human capabilities, we require divine help. Yes, destiny exists, but it is not everything. With sincerity and divine assistance, it is possible to alter the course of one's fate.

TWENTY-SIX

A *Mudang's* Special Dreams

Mudangs dream much more than the average person. They not only dream during their sleep at night but also witness dream-like visions during their waking hours. Since these visions carry meaning, none should be overlooked or taken lightly.

When I went to perform in the United States, the Korean Shamanic *gut* ritual was not widely recognized or acknowledged. However, three years after my performance in the United States, I received the designation of National Intangible Cultural Property as the Bearer of the *Seohaean Baeyeonshin-gut* and *Daedong-gut*.[100] This recognition resulted from fifteen years of relentless performances and participation in the National Folk Art Performance Contest.

At first, when my troupe performed in the United States, we received little attention or recognition. Despite being the most

---

100. 서해안 배연신굿 및 대동굿, the Abundant Fishing & Village Ritual of the West Sea.

experienced and seasoned performers, we were always overshadowed when introduced to the audience. While other performers
held prestigious titles as Bearers of National Intangible Cultural
Property or were respected as "masters" in the National Dance
Company, we began with no official titles or designation. Even so,
we always performed with joyful hearts.

However, there were still times when we felt disheartened by
prejudice and narrow-mindedness. It seemed that my discour-
agement had been conveyed to the gods. One day, in a dream,
an elderly grandfather spirit with white hair appeared. His beard
flowed down to his chest, and he invited me to sit before him.

"I have come to take care of you. Do not worry."

The grandfather performed a *shinsataekil*[101] on a clean sheet
of paper and wrote down the date with a brush. He then told me to
bow in front of it.

"But this is the United States. Where would a *gut* be
performed?" I asked.

Still, I followed the grandfather's instructions and bowed
deeply before the dated paper.

"Just wait," he said.

After saying those words, the grandfather disappeared. The
following morning, when I woke up from the dream, an uncon-
trollable surge of divine energy coursed through me. I gathered
scattered clothes and towels, draping them on my back and tying
them around my waist, and began dancing. During my dance, I
entered the neighboring room where an elderly female dancer slept
and awakened her. The grandmother gathered up her own disrobed
clothes, draped them on her body, and even placed a torn stocking
on her head to dance with me. Gradually, people from other rooms
joined, transforming the scene into a wild and ecstatic dance party.

---

101. 신사택일, a Shamanic practice of selecting an auspicious day for a ritual.

Observing this spectacle, members of other performance groups inquired what was happening.

"Why are we dancing? Who told us to dance?"

Still, the dancers looked at one another and began to dance tirelessly without understanding why.

"Just wait and see," I said. "Tomorrow, we will have the opportunity to perform a grand *gut*."

"Who has invited us to perform such a significant *gut?*"

"Grandfather Spirit!"

Their faces expressing a mix of faith and skepticism, the dancers unleashed divine energy through wild movements. The next day, our group went to a restaurant to have a meal and met a man named Cheon O-Seong, who was working at the New York Consulate. Surprisingly, he offered us a significant proposal. He invited us to perform a *gut* at an event organized by The Asia Society. The *gut* performers, who had danced together the previous day, exchanged bewildered glances filled with joy and astonishment. It might be hard to believe, yet it truly happened.

The dreams of *manshins* are special—dreams that can feel like reality, while the reality of a *manshin* can unfold like a dream. A *manshin's* dreams are dreamed even during a *gut*, visions often unfolding like a film is playing. Divine Spirit and gods appear and provide guidance in dreams when there are important matters to pay attention to.

A long time ago, I performed a *Jaesu-gut* for a household engaged in business. After invoking and paying respect to the deities, just as I was about to begin the *gut*, I saw a young bachelor spirit with disheveled hair and water dripping from his head enter the ritual space. During different passages of a *gut*, a *mudang* can see the various spirits coming and going. Especially in the opening passage, during the invocation, when all the relevant spirits for the *gut* are invited, many different deities come and gather around. At the same time, the ancestral spirits of the household also arrive.

The belated bachelor spirit with disheveled hair wore a soiled traditional *jeogori*, and his body was drenched in water. I called the mistress of the home and asked if they had any ancestors who had died by drowning as a bachelor before the age of thirty, and she said no. I performed another passage of the *gut* and asked again.

"He has a round face but looks rather tough, and his clothes are worn out."

Then the daughter-in-law, seated next to the mistress, tapped her knee and exclaimed, "Oh my, do even cousins come during the *gut?* From how you describe him, it's my older cousin who drowned. You speak as if you've really seen him." After that, the daughter-in-law kept stealing curious glances at me.

Before the passage for ancestral spirits, I took a moment to rest privately in another room. Suddenly, my body felt itchy, and I was overwhelmed with sleepiness. Wondering what dream I might have, I lay down to rest when a tall man with a dark complexion appeared right in front of me.

"It looks like you're almost through with the *gut,* and you dare not recognize me—ignoring me instead? Look at me! See who I am!" The man shouted and then sat down, vigorously beating a drum and the gong.

Startled, I woke up only to find that the man had vanished, and instead, my spirit aunt, who had accompanied me to the *gut,* and her spirit daughter were resting nearby.

"Ah, what a strange dream."

"Hey, you didn't even sleep, so what dream could you have had?" my spirit aunt, who cherished me, casually retorted.

It was clear that this was no ordinary dream. Significant dreams could occur even during brief moments of sleep. I asked my aunt to fetch the mistress of the house. If we neglected to pay respects to important ancestral spirits before completing the *gut*, all our previous efforts could be in vain.

I shared my dream with the mistress, earnestly imploring her to carefully consider if there were any ancestral spirits we had failed to honor. While the mistress maintained her ignorance, it seemed to me that there was more to the situation.

"Please do not deceive me. We are offering this *gut* to honor and show respect to your ancestors for the sake of their descendants. However, if we overlook an ancestral spirit, the *gut* will have been for nothing." I solemnly explained one more time. "Please think it through carefully."

Only then did the mistress let out a long sigh. "It must be my late husband."

She explained that her elderly husband had been a *mudang* during his lifetime. In his younger days, he had attended a funeral, and on his way back, near the Samgak Mountains, spirits descended upon him. Suddenly, he fell backward and started babbling while the friends traveling with him could only watch in astonishment. Then the man, who appeared to be unconscious, suddenly rose up, shouted loudly, and rushed to uproot a large boulder. He dug beneath the rock with his bare hands. Beneath the rock was a Shamanic rattle and a warrior's sword wrapped in cotton cloth. After that, her husband suffered severely from spirit illness until he eventually underwent the *Naerim-gut* initiation ritual.

Her late husband was renowned for his precise divinations, so there was never a shortage of clients in his home. With the money he earned, he sent his eldest son to study abroad in Japan and ensured that the rest of his children completed their university education. However, his wife and other family members felt immense embarrassment that he was a *baksu mudang*—a male shaman—and they all lived in secrecy and shame. Naturally, the man didn't receive proper recognition and care from his children even after death. He was likely deeply resentful.

I gently admonished his family members, emphasizing the importance of sincerely comforting and honoring their father and husband's spirit, regardless of their past failure to do so. The two sons shed hot tears and tightly gripped my hands. We made an offering of freshly steamed rice cakes and devotedly dedicated a whole passage of the *gut* to the man who had appeared in my dream. The mistress, overwhelmed with emotions, prostrated herself and did not get up for a very long time. The entire family held onto their father's spirit, sincerely repented, and wept. The brief dream of the *mudang* had allowed the family to reclaim and reconnect with a forgotten ancestor.

TWENTY-SEVEN

If Only I Could Bring Attention to the *Gut*

As my *gut* performances gained wider recognition, I began receiving various requests to appear on television. Not only that, but thanks to my acclaimed *gut* rituals, I also had the opportunity to appear in both movies and TV dramas. While filming the movie *Seoul Manshin*, I had the pleasure of crossing paths with actress Kim Ji-Mi. Kim Ji-Mi portrayed the character of the *manshin* in the film, and there was considerable buzz surrounding her lead role.

I tutored Kim Ji-Mi in the art of dancing and performing a *gut*. While she often portrayed high-maintenance and haughty roles in films, in real life, she was more like a down-to-earth warrior. She also displayed sweet devotion and love as a daughter. In one scene, she grills a large corvina and delicately places fish meat on her mother's spoon, saying, "Mother, you must eat well." I found this the most beautiful of any of her movie scenes. Although there were rumors that Kim Ji-Mi underwent a *Naerim-gut* ritual, they were false. The truth was that she performed a *gut* because she fell seriously ill while filming another movie, *Biguni*.[102] While she had considered the possibility that she had a spirit illness and required a *Naerim-gut*, she confirmed that wasn't the case.

For the premiere of KBS TV Literary Theater's *Baettaragi*, I was given the opportunity to portray a shaman. The story revolves around a fisherman who goes missing at sea and a female protagonist who tragically takes her own life after being falsely accused of infidelity by her abusive husband. The role of the female lead was played by Jang Mi-Hee, the most popular actress at the time. I portrayed the character of a *mudang*, who performs a *Neokgeoji-gut* for the drowned seaman.

The *Neokgeoji-gut* is a ritual that retrieves the soul of a person who drowned. A fowl is released into the water where the drowning took place for the deceased's soul to attach to before the fowl returns to the shore. When the deceased is male, a hen is released; when the deceased is female, a rooster is sent into the water. As the fowl is released into the water, a song is sung to comfort the deceased's spirit.

In the film, the fowl was released into the sea while I performed calling out for the soul.

> *"Today, we offer a gut to retrieve the soul of the one who died*
> *at sea.*
> *We invoke the sacred name of the departed soul,*
> *We invite you to return, riding the fowl from the under-*
> *water realm.*
> *The grieving family implores the deceased*
> *to heed the sound of gongs and drums and join this gut.*
> *They prepared clothes and shoes, even money for the travel*
> *to the afterlife.*

---

102. 비구니, a female Buddhist nun.

Follow the waves, accept our blessings, and emerge
onto the land.
The family eagerly awaits, longing to meet the
departed spirit,
diligently searching and waiting.
Upon hearing our plea, please come forth before
time runs out.
We beseech all underwater gods and spirits to clear the path
and assist this unfortunate, unjustly departed soul.
O, departed soul, come forth!"

This scene was filmed on the second day of the first Lunar month on Kanghwa Island, and the sea was white with frost—so cold that even breathing caused ice to form in the nostrils. The film crew was out at sea on a boat, where producer Shim Hyun-woo took care of various details and meticulously directed the film.

When it was my turn to step before the camera, people were waiting on the beach, prepared for any emergency that might arise. It was a precaution they took due to the frigid seawater. With cameras rolling, I received a signal from the director and jumped into the sea with the hen in my arms. Then I mournfully chanted for the drowned man and slowly released the hen into the water. Perhaps thanks to the protection and help of Spirit, I managed to film my scene in just one take. The ritual dress I wore became heavy and soaked in seawater, and my body was freezing. As I trudged onto the sandy beach, I saw my older sister wailing in sorrow.

"Why do you choose to suffer like this? What glory or honor awaits you in this pain?" she asked.

In truth, my body was so tense I hadn't even noticed the biting cold as I plunged into the water. However, my sister, who watched me closely, felt differently. She felt pity for her younger sister, who faced daily hardships and received little recognition, now enduring bitter winter cold.

Kim Nan-Young and other actors portraying the mourners on the beach wailed even louder when they saw my sister crying so sorrowfully. Later, I learned that due to my sister's deeply mournful cries, they mistakenly believed that I had actually retrieved a soul and that my sister was the deceased's family. *Baetarragi* was broadcast on TV later and received favorable reviews, serving as an opportunity for me to popularize the *gut* among the general public.

Still, sometimes I found myself wondering, just as my sister did, for what glory or honor did I choose to plunge into the biting cold sea and endure such suffering? It wasn't for fame or popularity. It was simply my one earnest desire, my hope that many people would have the opportunity to witness and appreciate our *gut* ritual. That was the only heartfelt wish I had.

TWENTY-EIGHT

A *Mudang* is a Doctor Who Heals Ailments of the Heart

There are times when a *mudang* must become a doctor. While physicians treat physical ailments, *mudangs* treat ailments caused by spirits. These sicknesses, hidden in the deep recesses of the body, can only be cured by relying on the power of a *mudang.*

Early in the summer of 1993, I had a dream at dawn in which I saw myself standing on a high cliff. I was barely balancing on the edge of the rock, teetering precariously over unfathomable depths. Nervous and trembling, I mustered the courage to leap across to the other side. Even a slight misstep would have sent me plunging into the abyss, but before I knew it, I was walking freely in a vast and lush plain. I wandered through the grassy field with a free, light heart until I woke up.

Perhaps because of that dream, I eagerly anticipated calls from my clients. It was only later in the afternoon when the telephone rang loudly, jolting me to pick it up. A deep masculine voice came through the other end of the line.

"I'm calling because I would like your counsel. My child..."

As the man spoke, I blurted out, "Your child is at the hospital. In the intensive care unit?"

The man was stunned and quickly replied, "Yes." It was evident that he was taken aback.

Sometimes, the spirits inform me of certain events in advance through dreams. By interpreting these dreams, I can easily discern what will happen that day. I had spent the day contemplating the vision I'd had at dawn and preparing myself.

The child who was hospitalized was an eight-year-old boy. He had a seizure and collapsed while playing video games, leading to his admission to the intensive care unit. Despite being prescribed strong medication and receiving treatment, he was unable to sleep and experienced tremors throughout his body. This incident even made it on the TV news. The child had been in the hospital for two months without any improvement. He had been examined by various departments, including pediatrics, internal medicine, and psychiatry, and had undergone numerous tests, but the cause of his illness remained unknown. The doctors could only assure the parents that they were doing their best. Then one of the doctors, feeling frustrated, muttered to himself, "Perhaps he needs a *gut*," shaking his head. At their wits' end, the child's parents contacted me after inquiring to others.

I felt the confidence bestowed upon me by the spirits in my dream, and the vast, bright meadow shimmered before my eyes.

"Are you willing to do as I ask? You must have faith that your child will improve."

"Yes, I will do whatever you ask." The father's voice was filled with desperation.

"Go to a farm, buy a young hen, and wrap it in the child's

clothes. Trim the child's bangs, fingernails, and toenails, then wrap the clippings around the hen's ankles," I instructed. "Then take eight grains of rice, wrap them in a navy cloth, and rub that on the child's lips."

I continued to explain the intricate ritual in detail. "Purchase hemp cloth and divide into twelve strips, then tie them around the hen, securing them with twelve knots. Place nine plates of rice, one plate of soybean paste, and one plate of salt in the room, and offer your prayers before them. Pray sincerely and say: *We offer this live hen in place of our child as a daesudaemyeong ritual. He is at the hospital, and we ask for the restoration of his health and clarity of his mind before it is too late.*"

Finally, I instructed him to place the prepared hen and the plates of offerings at a three-way crossroad, facing a non-haunted direction, before offering prayers once more and then returning home without looking back. After that, I told him to observe any changes in the child over the next two to three days.

On the third day, the phone rang.

"How is the child?" I asked.

"He has improved but cries whenever he sees his mother."

The child, who had regained consciousness, shed tears whenever he saw his mother. Moved with compassion, his mother asked what he wanted to eat, but he just stared at her without responding. Recalling what the child liked, his mother suggested, "Shall we give you yogurt?" At that, the child nodded. His mother managed to feed him yogurt through a rubber hose, but after that, the nurse prohibited her from entering the hospital room, citing interference with his treatment.

"He is starting to improve, so follow the prescription I gave you one more time," I said.

The child's father agreed to follow my instructions, but after that, there was no news for a whole week. Finally, the child's father called again.

"What should we do? We still don't know the exact diagnosis, and the doctors keep saying they're doing their best."

"Will you trust me one last time?" I asked him. "This time, we should hold a *gut*."

As always, bringing up the idea of performing a *gut* is difficult. Most people doubt the effectiveness of a *Byeong-gut*—an illness ritual—instead believing that only doctors can cure illnesses, while *guts* are considered superstitions. However, perhaps because the child's condition showed improvement, the father agreed to trust me and hold a *gut*.

On the day of the *gut*, the child's mother also attended. She was a devout Catholic, which is why I had been in contact with the boy's father all this time. However, driven by their desperate hope to save their child, we all wholeheartedly participated in the *gut*. While performing the ritual, I had a strong intuition and a positive feeling that the child would recover and regain his health. Fortunately, after the *gut*, the child started showing signs of improvement. He recognized his parents and even reacted by frowning when they pinched him. The child was transferred to a regular hospital unit.

However, just ten days later, I received yet another call from his parents. The child would not open his eyes and had returned to a state of unconsciousness.

"The doctors are advising us to brace for the worst. What should we do?"

"The child will get better. You have decided to trust me, so please have faith until the end! Let the child sleep to his heart's content," I said. "Why is everyone making such a fuss over a sleeping child?" I spoke firmly.

Since the boy hadn't eaten for a long time, I suggested feeding him bone broth through a tube but otherwise leaving him alone. The mother began calling me once every three days. Whenever the doctor said anything, she would spiral and lose her grounding.

"They said there's no hope. Should we really just leave him as he is?"

"Have faith and wait. It's not me who will make him better, but the divine power of *Dangun Sanshin*,[103] so please have faith."

The most important aspect of healing the sick is faith. The caretaker or the person providing treatment must possess genuine trust and confidence in the possibility of healing. This belief and its assurance are conveyed to the patient, enabling the patient to maintain the will to recover.

The mother's voice, so overcome with anxiety, gradually brightened. She observed improvements in her child's complexion and noted that he was gaining weight, even while asleep. The child continued to sleep for approximately twenty days. He occasionally opened and closed his eyes, and just as he was about to develop bedsores on his back, he woke up with a radiant face. The doctors were astonished, and the parents were overwhelmed with joy.

After being discharged, the boy no longer showed interest in video games and fully returned to his previous state of health. He did well in school and frequently visited my home with his mother. Even to this day, on special days such as *Ipchun* or *Chilseok*, they remember and pay me a visit.

The child's ailment was not simply physical but rather an illness caused by ghosts or evil spirits. The child had excessively indulged in electronic games, severely disrupting the natural

---

103. 단군산신, Dangun was the founding father of ancient Korea as shown in the Dangun Myth, and it is said he later went into the mountains and became a Sanshin, Mountain God.

energy flow in his body. Moreover, the child had unknowingly engaged in activities forbidden by spirits, which led to the manifestation of the illness. Therefore, his was not a disease that could be treated by doctors.

The *Byeong-gut* illness ritual is essential. Just as doctors cannot cure all diseases, performing a *gut* does not guarantee recovery from every illness. However, some illnesses require a *gut* in order for allopathic medication or treatment to be effective. Addressing both the spirit and the body, a *Byeong-gut* plays a crucial role in managing one's overall health.

TWENTY-NINE

The Six Rituals of Hwanghae Province

Despite seeking refuge and settling in the South after the war, my *gut* rituals have been praised for preserving the authentic form of North Korean *guts*. Since they are passed down orally and physically from person to person, it is challenging to preserve their original form. I believe it is not desirable for a *manshin* to significantly alter the original content of the *gut* based on their opinions or biases. This may be why I have dedicated so much effort to preserving and documenting the *gut* rituals of my hometown in Hwanghae Province.

There are six main types of *Hwanghae-guts*. These include the *Cheolmuri-gut*, performed to promote individual health and prosperity; the *Baeyeonshin-gut*, *Jinogwi-gut*, and *Mansudaetak-gut*—each serving their own specific purpose—and the *Daedong-gut*, which is performed to foster harmony and prosperity within a village. Additionally, a *Naerim-gut* is also conducted to help people afflicted with spirit illness become a *mudang*.

The *Cheolmuri-gut*, meaning "gatherings (*muri*) of people following seasons (*cheol*)," is performed for the prosperity of a household. It is conducted in homes with no significant misfortune and simply aims to foster success in a family's health and business. It is usually held once every three years, and the ideal timing for the ritual is on the sacred first or tenth Lunar months.

The *Baeyeonshin-gut* is performed in households relying on fishing for their livelihood and prays for fishermen's safety and abundant catches. This *gut* is traditionally performed on the western coast, with the most common timing being in the first three Lunar months.

The *Jinogwi-gut* is performed to console the spirit of the dead and to pray and bless their heavenly journey. It is commonly conducted during *Samuje*[104] or within the year of a person's passing. Usually, if there is a deceased person in a household, no other *guts* are performed for three years except for the *Jinowgi-gut*. This is because it is believed that the spirit of the deceased takes away all the offerings and benefits from *guts*.

A *Mansudaetak-gut* is performed for the longevity and well-being of an elder and, while the elder is still alive, for their ascent to the heavenly path after death. This *gut* aims to open a path to a favorable afterlife before one has passed and consists of a large-scale ceremony over five days. It is mainly performed in high-ranking noble, economically-affluent households.

A *Daedong-gut* is performed for the well-being and prosperity of an entire village. Although there may be slight variations between villages, it is typically conducted once every three years—although some villages hold it annually. On the first three days of the first Lunar month, the date of the *gut* is divined, and the ritual is then conducted for three to five days during the first

---

104. 삼우제, a ritual honoring the deceased after three days of mourning.

full moon. It is a true community ritual in which the entire village prepares and participates, fostering harmony and unity within the community.

The *Naerim-gut* is an initiation ritual, a *mudang gut* that a person suffering from spirit sickness receives through another *manshin*—a solemn Shamanic procedure that must be undergone to become a *mudang*. In the past, there were three separate *guts*: the *Heoju-gut*,[105] *Naerim-gut*, and *Soseul-gut*,[106] performed for a person to be recognized as a genuine *mudang*. The ritual has been simplified these days, and a *Naerim-gut* is performed in combination with the *Heoju-gut* and *Soseul-gut*. The person who receives the *Naerim-gut* not only recovers from spirit sickness but also gains qualifications to begin receiving training as a *mudang*.

When I used to go watch *guts* as a child, I could spend the whole day engrossed, unaware of the passing time. In my hometown of Hwanghae Province, rituals were filled with wit and humor. At first glance, the *gut* appeared to be a bustling and lively carnival, but the true essence was utmost devotion to the deities. Whenever there was a *Cheolmuri-gut*, the neighborhood transformed into a festive atmosphere, the performers pounding blessings and good fortune into the mortars with bawdy and witty humor. A mischievous woman would pretend to steal from the *gut* altar and then accuse spectators of being thieves, creating playful and humorous situations. A blind man would approach any woman and say, "Sis, let me hold your wrist," and the woman responded, "Here you go," before handing him a *janggu* drumstick. The blind man would play dumb and say, "Sis, how much did you miss me that your wrist has become as thin as a bamboo stick?" Another scene involved

---

105. 허주굿, a ritual of clearing evil or unnecessary spirits from the shaman-to-be.

106. 솟을굿, a ritual of activating and energizing the gods for a newly initiated shaman to do their work successfully.

a father and son working the mortars, with the son speaking disrespectfully to his father, forgoing honorific language, and then turning to the crowd.

"Hello there, guests. Please do not spoil your sons just because they're boys, for he will soon disregard his own father and talk back to him."

This act served as a reminder to not overly favor sons and to prioritize the proper upbringing of all children. *Guts* provided occasions for neighbors to share their thoughts and express requests they wanted to make to each other. As long-repressed conversations and appeals flowed out, there were also raunchy and awkward scenes, such as "Do you know if your mother still enjoys sex?" and "How should I know what she does with her own body?" However, reflecting on it now, I realize that even sexual desires were not concealed or repressed but transformed into amusing entertainment and stories. Such intimate ritual performances are experienced only in Hwanghae; other regions do not know of or hold such *guts*. Perhaps it's better that way, as it could lead to misunderstandings.

THIRTY

Gut: A Festival Between Humans and Spirits

A *gut* is at once a spirited celebration and a tearful catharsis. Those who have never witnessed a *gut* call it fearful, but that is because they do not understand it. With a colorful array of fruits and delectable rice cakes, accompanied by spirited dancing and entertaining songs, it's hard to find a celebration that rivals a *gut*. A *gut* is a grand festival where spirits and humans come together like friends, mingling like daughters and sons, laughing and crying until the day breaks. As the celebration unfolds, human sorrows and *han* are dissolved. Both the bitterness harbored by humans and the bitterness of the gods, enraged by human foolishness, are released. The spirits, who have become like friends, alleviate the deep-seated pain and *han* within humans, much like snow melting on a spring day. As a friend, can you ignore someone when they are in pain or distress if you have just danced and played with them? The deities, too, are tender-hearted and compassionate. They resemble the warm and empathetic nature of the Korean people.

A *gut* isn't necessary to address the small, lingering wounds accumulated in daily life. You can confide in friends, have a drink, or sing your heart out in a karaoke room. Through these activities, you may find relief from your distressing emotions. However, there are times when you cannot heal your wounds on your own, no matter how hard you try. When you have experienced something incredibly traumatic or a wound runs so deep that it continues to bleed and fester in your heart, reaching a point where you cannot even comprehend where things began to go wrong, you need the help of the spirits. These deep and profound wounds must be identified, the festering pus must be removed, and the wounds must be adequately dressed to prevent further infection. Without taking these steps, a person may descend into even deeper affliction and suffering.

A *gut* is a gathering of gods and spirits together and seeking their help, rooted in the belief that with the assistance of deities, everything can be healed. Gods possess much more wisdom and power than we can imagine. That is why, when we are tormented by problems that seem hopeless, we turn to the spirits for guidance. However, the gods are not unconditionally on the side of humans. Some are enraged and dismayed by the arrogance and foolishness of humans. Therefore, before we can resolve our own *han*, we must address the grievances in the hearts of the gods. That is why we dance, sing, prepare rice cakes and fruits, and make sincere offerings to appease and soothe the spirits. We can only move the spirits' hearts through our sincere devotions and heartfelt intentions.

A *mudang* serves as a mediator between gods and humans, dancing and singing on behalf of the people, becoming like flowers and butterflies in the presence of the spirits. The *mudang* wholeheartedly and joyfully undertakes these actions to alleviate the sickened hearts of those suffering.

The *gut* is also a traditional practice of ancestral worship in which ancestors are held in deep reverence. How beautiful is it that through a *gut*, one can reunite with their departed fathers and mothers, opening a path for the ancestral spirits to interact with their beloved children and other descendants? These ancestors, who receive devoted care from their descendants, become protective guardians that shield against misfortune and bestow blessings upon future generations. In honoring and embracing ancestors, *guts* also instill in children the virtue of respecting their elders.

A *gut* is about sharing blessings, virtues, and food. During seasons when food was scarce and many people went hungry, community-wide *guts* were deliberately organized. The abundance of food from wealthy households was generously distributed to feed people from one village to another. A *Daedong-gut* was often held for this purpose.

The *Daedong-gut* is a ritual organized and carried out through the community's collective effort. An entire village comes together through this gut, praying for well-being, peace, and freedom from conflicts. It was believed that only when a village is peaceful can individuals find peace. For this reason, instead of solely wishing for individual blessings, there is a tradition of sharing food and blessings widely, with a sense of kinship and solidarity.

The *gut* is a comprehensive art form. Those who have witnessed *gut* ceremonies are amazed by it. They wonder how Shamanic attire can be so diverse and vibrant in color. The white *jangsam*, the blue *jeonbok* coat for the Warrior God, the yellow *mongduri* robe for the *Daeshin* Goddess, the green silk *wonsam* robe, the red and blue *gwandi* uniform attire, and more. Just wearing one of these garments is beautiful, but layering two or three creates a harmonious ensemble that is truly remarkable. Furthermore, the white triangular *goggal* hat, the colorfully bejeweled *jokduri* headpiece, the red and blue sashes, and various other adornments are incredibly exquisite. A foreign woman who studies fashion once lavishly praised these garments and accessories as utterly unique and beautiful, unlike anything she had ever seen in this world.

The same goes for food. *Gut* ceremonies are overflowing with traditional food. There are mouthwatering sweet red bean rice cakes, colorful rice cake balls, vibrant red apples, pears, various fruits, sweet and chewy jujubes, and well-ripened chestnuts. All these foods are grown and harvested from the Earth's bounty. How can the spirits not be moved by offering such food with utmost sincerity?

Lastly, an essential aspect of the *gut* is that it does not promote or facilitate revenge. The *gut* teaches forgiveness and compassion. Korean people are inherently kind-hearted. Even when hurt by others, they do not seek retaliation. Instead, they often bury the pain in their hearts and endure, only to release and soothe the deep-seated *han* and pain through participating in a *gut*. To those who may consider such endurance foolish or naïve, it is not. Seeking revenge only perpetuates a cycle of vengeance and fuels greater anger. However, by nurturing forgiveness and reconciliation, by releasing the accumulated bitterness to the vast skies and deep seas, the anger dissipates and never returns. It is a way of navigating this world with a more expansive heart while embracing generosity and abundance.

When life feels enshrouded in darkness—becomes unbearably difficult and torturous—and the next steps are invisible, that's when engaging in a lively *gut* becomes most crucial. How blessed it is to release such deep-seated pain in the presence of the spirits and feel revitalized in the heart as if one has been reborn.

Kim Keum-Hwa during a West Sea Abundant Fishing & Village Ritual at Inchon, circa 2000.

Previous page: Kim Keum-Hwa during a *Jaesu-gut* in 1995. The ritual was for prosperity and blessing for the client's family.

Kim Keum-Hwa had a deep desire to preserve traditional *gut* rituals and pass them down to future generations. She participated in countless performances to introduce the dance and music of the *gut* rituals in her lifetime.

Kim Keum-Hwa performing a ritual at Dr. Zo Zayong's
Emile Museum in 1981.

Previous page: *Gut* is not only a practice of ancestral and spirit worship, but also
a comprehensive art form of dance, music, and storytelling.

As Kim gained more recognition, more people interested in Korean Shamanism and ancient traditions from all over the world sought her out.

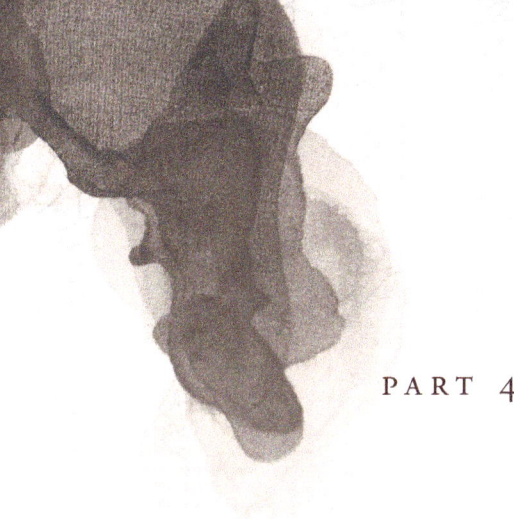

PART 4

A Lonely Path,
A Mudang's Path

A long way to go with no end in sight.
But just keep following me along the endless path.
Along the way, there will be rocky cliffs and thorny bushes.
There will be mountains to climb and oceans to cross.
Face every trial, endure, and overcome them.

by Kim Keum-Hwa

THIRTY-ONE

Keep Rising, No Matter How Many Times You Fall

I first became a spirit mother at the age of nineteen. Receiving a spirit daughter—a disciple—at that age, I was considered to have matured and succeeded faster than others. Back then, my nickname was *One Day Manshin* or *Hong Gil-dong*[107] *Manshin* because I quickly received and acquired messages from the spirits.

My first disciple was a fourteen-year-old girl named Yong-Hae. Yong-Hae had an extra finger at the end of her left pinky, making her six-fingered. One spring morning, I heard our dog barking loudly, so I went outside and found a scrawny girl standing in front of the gates of my house, her fists tightly clenched. It wasn't raining, but she was completely soaked and trembling. That was the first time I saw Yong-Hae.

Yong-Hae told me she had followed a grandfather who appeared to her in a dream all the way to my house. When she arrived at my house at dawn, the gods had already descended

107. 홍길동, a fictional folk hero of Korea with great skills and power.

upon her. While drinking the water my mother handed her, she suddenly stood up, gritted her teeth, and started jumping around the room.

"Eh-hey, how offensive! I followed the divine path, the path of the water, all the way here to become a great *mudang*. The gods are standing before and behind me, guiding me. So why don't you accept me at once and receive them?"

In truth, the person called to be a *mudang* was actually Yong-Hae's mother. When Yong-Hae's mother lived in her hometown, the spirits had descended upon her. However, she decided she would rather die than become a *mudang*, so she fled the village with her daughter Yong-Hae. But the destiny she thought she had escaped ultimately fell upon her own daughter. I felt such compassion for the tragic fate of Yong-Hae and her mother that I embraced Yong-Hae and wept with her.

In the end, Yong-Hae received a *Naerim-gut*. At that time, the relationship between a spirit mother and daughter was akin to that of a real mother and daughter, perhaps even stricter, with a more profound sense of responsibility. The preparation for the *Naerim-gut* was carried out by the spirit mother, and money was needed to gather various grains and food for the *gut*. However, I was just a nineteen-year-old young shaman. Yong-Hae's family also struggled to make ends meet and could not afford the expenses of the *gut*. So I swallowed my pride and went around the neighborhood begging for grains. Despite having walked with my head held high after becoming a *mudang*, I temporarily set aside my dignity for the sake of poor Yong-Hae.

Thanks to my neighbors' help, Yong-Hae was able to have a *Naerim-gut*. On the day of her ritual, all of us cried. The villagers who came to watch, the old woman who played the *janggu* drum, my family members, Yong-Hae's mother, and I—all of us weeping, feeling sorry for young Yong-Hae.

Yong-Hae, who was as tall as me, danced as gracefully as a butterfly. We stuck close together like sisters and friends and performed *gut* rituals together. Because we were always together and had a similar style of dancing and performing *guts*, they called me "the big one" and Yong-Hae "the little one." I skillfully performed *guts* like an experienced *manshin*, and Yong-Hae, who had recently received the gods, was accurate and precise in her divinations. As a result, we were warmly welcomed wherever we went.

Yet, within a year, I was cruelly separated from Yong-Hae. The war had broken out, scattering us in different directions. Every time I had to move due to the turmoil of the war, I tried to garner news about Yong-Hae, but I couldn't find any information. While fleeing to southern Korea, I cried an ocean of tears thinking about Yong-Hae. She and I had cherished and held each other in deep compassion, even more than real sisters. Losing Yong-Hae felt like a piece of my own heart had crumbled into dust. If she had survived the war, I am sure she would have become a great *manshin* somewhere.

After Yong-Hae, many more disciples sought me out and became my spirit daughters over the years. There are even foreign spirit daughters who practice Korean Shamanism outside of Korea. Andrea, who received a *Naerim-gut* a few years ago, still calls and checks in on me from time to time. There are many things a *mudang* should teach her spirit daughters, keeping them close so that they may watch and learn. I feel bad that she lives too far away for me to teach her or give her proper attention, but I am thankful she is healthy and happy in her homeland, healed from the sickness that had once caused her so much pain.

One of my most memorable disciples was Chae Hiah, now

Hiah Park, who received the spirits while studying Shamanism in the United States. She is a highly educated spirit daughter of mine who majored in traditional Korean music at the prestigious Seoul National University and pursued graduate studies in dance ethnology and ethnomusicology at UCLA. While studying abroad in the United States, she experienced the spirit sickness without realizing it and suffered greatly for over a year. Eventually, she returned home to Korea because she felt a constant call to come back. While watching a video on the *guts* of Hwanghae Province at the Korea Arts & Culture Education Service, she trembled and shed a lot of tears. After that, she expressed her desire to meet with me, and, with the help of her university friend, Professor Choi Jong-Min, our meeting was arranged. It took place during the scorching heat wave of the summer in 1981.

The moment our eyes met for the first time, a shiver ran down my spine, and it felt as if electricity surged through my body, giving me chills and making my hair stand on end. The spirits had already descended upon Hiah, filling her to her shoulders, and the energy was powerful. It was her destiny to receive a *Naerim-gut*. She accepted her fate calmly as if she had already known.

On the day Hiah received her *Naerim-gut*, many people gathered. Renowned scholars and professors in the field of folk studies, as well as Shamanic photographer Kim Soo-Nam, were in attendance. There was significant interest in the exceptional Hiah. I still vividly recall her powerful voice as she delivered an oracle atop the *jakdu* blades during the ceremony.

"You rascals, who are your ancestors? Are you the heirs of Dangun or the bastards of Westerners?"

Having lived abroad for a long time, Hiah harshly scolded what she perceived as the spinelessness of the Korean people. Her terrifying rebukes and commanding *gongsu* were so forceful that I felt a bit abashed. She garnered significant attention from the media and public. The KBS TV station asked us to reenact her *Naerim-gut* ceremony at the Bohyeon Sanshin Shrine and broadcast it through a program called "KBS Monday Special." Several prestigious university hospitals invited her for various psychoanalytic examinations, and she even appeared in director Ha Myung-Joong's 1986 film, *Placenta*. Most importantly, I was grateful to witness a shift in perspective towards Shamanism and *mudangs*, an acknowledgment that spirits can even descend upon highly educated and accomplished individuals like her. Hiah continues to travel between the United States and Europe, researching Shamanism and actively engaging in performances and healing activities.

As a spirit mother, my heart is filled with affections for all my spirit daughters. Whether they are far away or close by, exceptional or ordinary, they are all precious disciples of mine who hold a special and tender place in my heart. I have daughters who elicit my sympathy for their underdevelopment, daughters who exhibit unwavering strength like sons, daughters who are so close that there are no barriers between us, daughters who constantly surprise me, daughters who provoke my frustration and shame, daughters who are eager to move forward quickly unlike in the past, daughters who make me proud, daughters who are cold and unfeeling, daughters who cry even when adorned in fine silk clothes, and others. Until I pass away, I must embrace and nurture all of these spirit daughters.

My teachings are meticulous yet strict. Acting as a mediator between the spirits and humans is difficult. How can one step onto a *gut* stage, engaging with the spirits, without fully mastering the sincere art of serving them through the *gut*? Even if one possesses the skills to perform the *gut* flawlessly, without a sincere heart, it will inevitably fall short of conveying the will of Divine Spirit to humans. That is why I push and urge my disciples to strive harder and wholeheartedly devote themselves to their craft.

In the past, young *manshins* were not even allowed to sit next to the great *manshin* when they dined at the table. Instead, they had to sit on the ground to eat. When their spirit mothers or teachers went to the outhouse, they had to quietly follow and vigorously rub straw together until their palms were practically on fire, then slip the straw through the cracks in the door for toilet paper. During *gut* ceremonies on cold winter days, they would hold the straw shoes of the great *manshin* to their chests to warm them up and help put them on. The social rules and regulations of the *mudangs* were as strict as those of the military.

Among disciples these days, some prioritize money and fame and even harbor thoughts of surpassing and outshining their own teachers and elders. I emphasize to my disciples the importance of cultivating character and integrity above all else.

"A *mudang* who prioritizes money is a fraud. Are you prepared to endure hardship and suffering? If you plan to look down on and criticize your teacher, don't receive a *Naerim-gut*," I firmly state.

I, too, am human, and sometimes I cannot control my emotions and end up speaking harshly. Consequently, misunderstandings arise. So when I find myself being perceived as a hard-hearted and demanding teacher, it brings me anguish and sadness. Yet, unlike turning socks inside out, it is impossible to fully expose my inner thoughts and heart.

I have one disciple of whom I am particularly fond. Even when I criticize and scold her, she always smiles and says, "Thank you, teacher." One day, I asked the reason behind her response.

"Teacher, aren't you scolding me because you believe in me and want me to improve?"

Upon hearing my disciple's words, I couldn't help but laugh. If this isn't wholehearted understanding, what is?

Before being a teacher, the spirit mother is, first and foremost, a fellow *mudang* who intimately knows the excruciating pain of the *mudang's* path. She knows how challenging and overwhelming it is to dedicate one's life to serving Spirit—and how frustrating it is to be unable to live life according to one's will. In my younger days, I often wept out of self-pity and resentment toward the life I had to lead. Perhaps these thoughts are the cause. Whenever I welcome a new disciple and perform a *Naerim-gut*, I inevitably cry while chanting the *mansebaji*.[108]

> *"I've come to give blessings; I've come from a lonely path.*
> *To open closed doors, come follow me.*
> *It's a rough and distant path.*
> *A long way to go with no end in sight.*
> *But just keep following me along the endless path.*
> *Along the way, there will be rocky cliffs and thorny bushes.*
> *There will be mountains to climb and oceans to cross.*
> *Face every trial, endure, and overcome them.*
> *Keep your gaze high and your thoughts deep as you walk.*
> *Weather through all storms and tire.*
> *You will tire and fall. When you fall, rise again.*
> *And when you rise, you will fall again. You must keep rising.*
> *Keep falling countless times and keep rising countless times.*
> *Keep falling and falling, and finally, you will find your place*
> * to stand."*

---

108. 만세받이/만수받이, a Shamanic song and rhythm used by the shamans of North Korea or the central, non-coastal region of South Korea, where they alternate verses and choruses back and forth.

It is the fate of the *mudang* to spend a lifetime caring for others and praying for their blessings, to the point where their bones are drained and bodies exhausted, yet they never receive the recognition they deserve. People only desperately cling to *mudangs* and Spirit in times of emergency and coldly turn away once their needs are fulfilled. *Mudangs* endure wounds from people, yet they never find solace in return. When the *gut* is over, and the remnants of hemp and cotton burned away, which *mudangs* have not shed tears at the fleeting emptiness of it all?

I hope that my disciples can understand, even just a little, the heart of the spirit mother who has no choice but to sternly teach them to "keep falling countless times and keep rising countless times" as they embark on a course that no one else can accompany, a path that is treacherous and full of thorns.

THIRTY-TWO

Mediator Between Spirits and Humans

A *mudang* serves as a mediator between spirits and humans, standing on the side of humans while interceding, persuading, and soothing the spirits. They convey the heartfelt wishes of the people to the spirits and receive and convey the will of the spirits to humans. A *mudang* becomes a child chosen by the gods, and in order to enter the realm of the gods, she must relinquish herself. She must partake in the gods' food, sleep as they do, and walk in their footsteps. Being a *mudang* entails living with one foot in the world of spirits, embracing the concerns of others as her own, and awakening people to discern right from wrong.

A *mudang* who must embrace the worries and suffering of others naturally becomes an intervenor. If I walk down the street and witness young people engaged in a physical fight, I intervene and attempt to stop them, even if that means putting myself at risk. I cannot simply walk away. If I encounter someone in pain who has collapsed on the street, I rush to the police station to seek help. I also lend my ear to people grappling with unresolved issues, sitting with them in their suffering. All of these aspects are inherent to my calling as a *mudang*.

What makes the *gut* rituals difficult for a *mudang* is that she must embrace the suffering of others. When channeling spirits with deep grievances or offering prayers on behalf of the sick, a *mudang* experiences intense sadness, sheds tears, and feels drained. *Mudangs* encounter significant challenges when channeling the ancestral spirits of others. Each ancestor has a unique personality, and it can be quite difficult for a *mudang* to become possessed by them and embody their characteristics. Some ancestors are crass and utter vulgarities, while others may pick fights with family members they had troubled relationships with during their lifetime. The *mudang* is caught in a dilemma, as speaking whatever the possessing spirit wants to convey may deeply hurt the feelings of family members. However, suppressing an ancestor's intended message may anger the spirit and cause trouble for the *mudang* herself. In my youth, I often found mediating between the perspectives of spirits and humans burdensome and perplexing. However, with experiences gained from each *gut* and wisdom earned from the trials and passages of life, I have gradually found a sense of ease in my heart and confidently carried out ancestral passages through *guts*.

Just like there are good and bad people, there are also good and bad *mudangs*. A good *mudang* considers everyone who comes to her as part of her family. She cares about those who have come to her for a *gut* or are in some other way connected to her. Most importantly, the results and effects of her practices are pure. In my own practice, I visit my shrine every morning with a purified heart to pray for those seeking my help.

Often, my prayers are as simple as:

"Please help the troubled son of the laundromat lady find peace of mind."

"Please assist the grandmother in Yangpyeong-dong, who has dementia, in regaining clarity of mind."

"Please ensure smooth governance of the country, alleviating the hardships of its citizens."

For households that weigh heavily on her heart, a proper *mudang* calls to inquire about their well-being and offers blessings to alleviate their worries. Through these actions, people come to trust and have faith in the *mudang*.

A bad *mudang* is only obsessed with making money, forcefully recommending *guts* to all her clients. If the client hesitates, she fabricates stories to push them to have the ritual. There is no genuine intention to support or help others; her sole focus is on financial gain. Such *mudangs* are despised by the gods and cannot remain on the spiritual path for long. Since they have betrayed the gods, it will be difficult for them to reap any benefits from performing a *gut*.

Divine Spirit doesn't offer anything for free. If we act righteously and pray with sincere devotion, we will receive blessings in proportion to our efforts. Even if those blessings are not immediate, coming even much later, a sincere *mudang* will surely be repaid. Conversely, if a *mudang* harbors evil thoughts and engages in wicked actions, those will also come back to her. The saying, "There is no end to evil, but there is an end to goodness," holds true.

Although some might find them easy to confuse, *mudangs* and fortune tellers differ. Fortune-tellers and psychics can only read fortunes but do not know how to perform *guts*. In my home in the Hwanghae region, such individuals were called *sinjang halmai*—referring to those who travel from house to house with a bundle, offering fortune-telling services and palm readings.

There are various types of *mudangs* as well. Among them, the main distinctions are between *Naerim mudang*[109] and *Seseup mudang*. *Naerim mudangs* are individuals upon whom spirits descend and become *mudangs* through the *Naerim-gut*. *Seseup mudangs* inherit their profession through their family lineage without directly receiving the spirit themselves.

Although my maternal grandmother was a *mudang*, the spirits descended upon me, so I am clearly a *Naerim mudang*—even though I didn't desire it, it was inexorably my destiny. Throughout the many times when being a *mudang* was so lonely and challenging that I wanted to quit, I have occasionally envied *Seseup mudangs*. While both are *mudangs*, *Seseup mudangs* seem freer to me somehow, unbound by gods. Moreover, their rituals, music, and forms of *gut* have been passed down through generations, enabling them to have a well-established system. I have felt envious that their family members also engage in the same profession, assuming they wouldn't feel so isolated and could support each other.

The effect of *guts* performed by *Naerim mudangs* can vary greatly depending on the *mudang's* abilities, so it is always nerve-wracking and challenging. It is essential to entertain and please the ancestral spirits and to channel sincere and brilliant blessings from the deities. Above all, the effects of the *gut* must be clear and pure for a client to be pleased and positively evaluate the *mudang*.

A *mudang* must never falter in her mind and always maintain self-discipline. Even in the coldest winter, she must bathe in cold water to invigorate and purify her body and mind. Hot water is considered lifeless, while cold water is alive. The willingness to wash in cold water signifies the sacrifice needed to serve the gods. The same level of care is required for food; a *mudang* cannot simply eat anything but must be discerning in her choices.

---

109. Also called *Gangshin-mu* (강신무).

To follow these teachings, I arise each dawn at 4:30 to start my day. After offering freshly drawn water at my shrine, I pray. Then, at 5:20, I take my morning exercise near the back entrance of Kyung Hee University. Rarely do I skip my morning regimen unless there are exceptional circumstances because I believe my body needs to be healthy to receive the spirits with more energy and perform a *gut* more effectively. Having befriended other old women and men who also exercise in the morning, sharing pleasantries and engaging in conversations is enjoyable.

I slowly jog back home after finishing my morning exercise around 7:40. On days I am not performing a *gut*, I eat a simple breakfast and take my time reading the newspaper. To fulfill my role as a dedicated *mudang*, I should understand what is happening in the broader world. I am convinced that only a well-rounded *mudang*, who is a lifelong learner, can truly help people.

The people who need my help are always those in difficult and dire situations. They are not individuals who can easily afford divination or *gut* ceremonies. Sometimes, a person's life is on the line, and other times, the livelihood and fate of a household hang in the balance. To become a *mudang* who can open closed doors and offer solace, one must pray with ever greater devotion and humble oneself as a disciple before Divine Spirit.

To become a great *mudang*, one must lose oneself. One must release her own pain, trials, and self-pity to pour evermore devotion into caring for and consoling others. A great *mudang* must unconditionally obey and follow the will of the spirits and never spiritually manipulate or deceive others. She must accept everything in a positive light and surrender herself with humility. Only then can one become a great *mudang*, entering into even greater realms of the spiritual world.

THIRTY-THREE

A Lonely Path,
A Weary Path

In the not-so-distant past, everyone was poor—both the family hosting the *gut* and the *mudang* conducting the *gut* were equally impoverished. There were times when a *gut* was performed with growling stomachs, when no one had enough to eat and eggs, which are now commonplace, were as precious as meat. Once, when I visited a home to perform a *gut*, they served a few fried eggs for breakfast. Nowadays, eggs have become so common that they don't make much of an impression, but back then, a fried egg was truly a delicacy among delicacies. As we gathered around that table, eating our rice, we kept eyeing the fried eggs. I, too, felt pleased while looking at them.

Surely, they will save some for me? I thought. *I'll finish this rice first and enjoy the egg.*

However, before I could finish my rice, a woman named Hwang, who played the *janggu*, quickly devoured the eggs. How disappointing! As the saying goes, I felt like a dog chasing a chicken that had flown up to the roof. It was absurd for me to say something about her eating fried eggs, yet it was also disheartening to simply let it go. While lingering in frustration, the spirit elder accompanying me to the *gut* reproached me.

"Hurry up and finish eating so we can start the *gut*," she said. "What can be so delicious that you must savor every bit? It's pointless to chase after illusions."

My face flushed, not from the elder's words, but because everyone's gaze suddenly focused on me. I reluctantly put down my spoon, but the woman playing the *janggu* looked at me as if nothing had happened.

During those days, food was the measure of love and generosity. We had to be highly attentive whenever we slaughtered a pig for a *gut*. Every type of rice cake, whether a steamed white rice cake, a rounded rice cake, a bean flour cake, a round flat cake, or a red bean rice cake, had to be divided equally, even if it was just a tiny amount. The meat had to be distributed evenly, even if it amounted to only 300 grams per person. Some particular clients would come back and return the meat they had been given, claiming they had received only fat. Reflecting on it now, it's enough to burst into laughter, but food was the currency of care back then.

When the *mudang* offered blessings, people complained that someone else was mentioned first or treated better because they had given more money. Some households felt slighted, saying they were given the *bok tteok*—a rice cake symbolizing blessings— last due to their poverty. As a result, if I paid more attention to the needier households, the better-off families would also complain.

"That household gave little but was treated so well, so we should do the same." It may seem petty and small-minded, but it also made the community even more humble and close-knit, without any pretenses. The *mudang* and the neighbors trusted and relied on each other, discussing even the most minor matters. It was a time overshadowed by poverty, yet purity and simplicity existed among us.

Even though *mudangs* shared blessings and fortunes with others through the *gut*, there was a time when they were subject to cruel and harsh treatment. During the Japanese colonial era, Japanese military authorities actively suppressed and rejected *mudangs* and *gut* rituals. My maternal grandmother was frequently summoned to the local police office for interrogation solely because she was a *mudang*. Unable to openly perform *guts*, she sought refuge in a riverside cave to carry out the rituals. Villagers would pretend to go fishing and intentionally wear shabby clothes to gather where the *gut* would occur. It was only late at night that my grandmother would return to the cave to retrieve the Shamanic instruments. However, police and military officers would persistently pressure and harass the *mudangs*, demanding they surrender their Shamanic instruments.

During the Korean War, *mudangs* were targeted for expulsion and eradication, labeled as "reactionaries who eat away at the spirit of the people." They were accused of muttering nonsense and wasting precious resources for their *guts* during times of scarcity, often enduring guns pressed against their throats.

The situation only worsened in the 1960s during the post-war wave of modernization. The New Village Movement inflicted the greatest pain on our traditional Shamanic practices. The *gut* was stigmatized and immediately deemed "superstition." All neighborhood and village shrines were destroyed, and households were prohibited from performing *guts*. If a *gut* was performed, the police quickly found out and raided the location, forcefully dragging the *mudangs* out as if they were pieces of luggage and desecrating their sacred instruments by stomping on them with their boots. Although the *mudangs* had done nothing wrong, they were subjected to verbal attacks, demeaning language, and indiscriminate abuse.

"You, take off your clothes! Are you really going to the police station dressed in your damned *mudang* clothes?" the police officers would shout. "Can't you hear me telling you to strip?"

The terrified host of the *gut* fled in fear, leaving the bewildered *mudang* to be taken to the police station to face even further degradation and abuse. Later on, even the sight of students in their dark uniforms would make me jump in surprise. Of course, bad *mudangs* exploited the spirits for financial gain, especially in times of great precarity and oppression, when many sought solace in fortune-telling and *guts*. Bad *mudangs* took advantage of these vulnerable individuals, causing chaos and confusion. However, it was foolish to oppress the entire Shamanic community because of the actions of a few.

Another challenge that was just as difficult was the conflict with other religions. In Shamanism, there is not much resistance to accepting other faiths, as we believe that just as there is divinity everywhere in this world, there are also many spirits in the heavenly realm. However, it appears that even now, it is quite challenging for Christianity to accept Shamanism.

Once, on *Samjitnal*, the third day of the third Lunar month, I climbed Mount Samgaksan to pray on the mountain. From below, I could hear a bustling crowd and voices chanting, "Lord, Lord." I thought they were passersby and waited, but more than ten people approached, forming a circle around me. I was besieged with my rice cakes, pig's head, and the fruits I had prepared. The people began clapping their hands and, after announcing a hymn number, started singing loudly. When their singing ended, they drew a cross on the pig's head, said, "Save this poor little lamb," and drew a cross on my back while shouting, "Hallelujah!"

"Excuse me, what are you doing, violently interrupting someone's prayer?" I couldn't bear it any longer and demanded an explanation.

"You are possessed by the devil's spirit. Hallelujah!" They completely ignored my words and went on to trample my incense and sprinkle water everywhere, desecrating my prayer ritual.

"Lord, guide this poor daughter of yours onto the right path. Amen!"

"Excuse me," I interrupted, "But I don't think the Lord you believe in would approve of your actions. Please leave."

Still, they could not be restrained. With more than ten people assailing one person, there was no way to fend them off. I couldn't help but feel sorry for them. Such behavior seemed to tarnish their own faith and bring shame to their god. I believe that gods and spirits do not desire humans to fight each other; that gods wish for all humans to live in peace with one another.

Even for renters, there is a rule for both landlords and tenants to coexist and respect each other. Regarding religion, it is not right to arrogantly judge and reject other religions as superstitions while insisting that only one's own faith is correct. Shamanism is also a legitimate religion, our traditional religious practice passed down through generations of Korean culture. It is inappropriate for any spiritual practitioner to automatically reject and ostracize others simply because they worship different gods.

Some people fear the vibrant flags, *jakdu* knives, and the *han*-ridden sorrowful wailing accompanying *gut* rituals. It is true that compared to the solemn and quiet worship in Christian churches, the lively atmosphere of the *gut*, with its loud drums, gongs, and the impassioned shouts of the *mudang*, may not easily captivate everyone. Yet this business of living, dying, and making life possible is not always tranquil. Life is naked pain and demands a resilient and hardened heart to endure its relentless hardships. *Musok*—Korean Shamanism—will continue flourishing as a living faith, providing unwavering support to those who navigate the treacherous twists and trials of human existence.

THIRTY-FOUR

Riding *Jakdu* Blades and Offering Oracles

Before becoming an official *mudang*, I used to play at riding *jakdu* blades. When the winter solstice and its cold eleventh Lunar month arrived, my mother would venture far away to sell goods from her bundle, ensuring our family didn't go hungry throughout the winter. I gathered my village friends at my house, and we played together. There weren't many activities for fun during that time, so I would often imitate my grandmother and play at performing *guts*.

My friends gathered in a circle in the small corner of the room while I stood in the middle to perform a *mudang* dance. One child would shake a bunch of seashells to match the rhythm, while another would clap their knees to provide the beats. I would feel an electrifying sensation running through my body in those moments, spinning and dancing so quickly that my feet barely touched the ground. But one day, after dancing for a while, I suddenly ran out of the room, grabbed the well-sharpened harvest sickle we kept under the eaves for the autumn harvest, and then returned. The blade shone blue in the light. I made the other kids hold the sickle properly, took off my socks, and stood on the blade. Balancing on the single blade of a sickle was difficult. Barefoot, I kept jumping on and off of it, dancing with the blade for a long time and offering my friends the oracles that poured out of my mouth.

"Your father will die around this time," I told one.

"Don't marry into that family; they will kick you out soon enough!" I advised another.

When I stepped off the blades after my trance-like play, I would find that only one or two children remained in the room. Initially, they had joined the play for fun, but as I started behaving more like a real *mudang*, most became frightened and fled.

A *gut* generally consists of twelve different passages, each associated with a specific god who possesses a distinct personality. Some deities enjoy dancing and singing, while others favor indulging in food, drink, and conversation. In the passage involving *jakdu* blades, the Warrior General God is the deity that descends upon the *mudang*, seeking to exhibit strength and dignity to the people. As a result, tasks such as riding the *jakdu* knives, challenging for ordinary individuals, are entrusted to the *mudang*, who serves as a disciple of Spirit. The intention is for people to recognize the Warrior God's power and might and treat the deity with utmost respect and reverence. Upon the gleaming *jakdu* blade, the *mudang* dances with the fervor of a warrior, loudly commanding and conveying the will of Spirit.

The *jakdu* blades are not placed directly on the ground but are mounted on top of a *chilseongdan*—the Seven Star, multi-layered altar. A mortar is placed at the bottom of the altar with one *mal* of white rice placed inside. To prevent the rice from moving, a flat pounding board is placed on top to secure it. On top of that sits a food table, a jug filled with water, and a square wooden board containing rice. The overall height of this seven-layered altar exceeds that of a person.

Building the *chilseongdan* signifies the Warrior God has reverence for *Chilseong-shin*, the Seven-Star Deity, and the water jug represents devotion to the *Yongwang-nim*, the Water God. After building the seven-layered altar, the *mudang* holds the long warrior swords in both hands and begins to invoke the Warrior Spirit. During this time, a cleansed individual diligently sharpens the *jakdu* blades until they are razor-edged. The person sharpening the ritual knives must not speak during the ritual, as it is considered impure, so a folded white paper called *hami* is placed in their mouth to prevent them from speaking.

After performing a dance that invites the gods into her body, the *mudang* mounts the *jakdu* blades. She may bring the pointed edges to her cheeks or tongue or glide them across her arms and legs. Then she firmly secures the two *jakdu* blades on the very top of the seven-layered altar. After washing her feet in clean water, she stands barefoot on the altar. At this moment, the rhythm of the Shamanic music intensifies. The *mudang* swiftly spins, vigorously jumps up and down, and eagerly awaits the deep descent of the spirit into her being. When her body begins tingling, her hair stands on end, and she feels like she is being lifted towards the sky by a powerful force, she leaps onto the *jakdu* blades. Once on the knives, she dances, engages in warrior play, and showcases a sword dance. Finally, she delivers oracles to the people.

Balancing on the *jakdu* blades requires stricter adherence to taboos than at any other time. If these boundaries are violated, the *mudang* may be unable to ride the knives or suffer cuts on her feet. It is crucial to guard the vicinity of the *gut* platform to prevent the entry of impure individuals or animals, and one must refrain from speaking impure or negative words. Above all, people must pray sincerely and offer their heartfelt devotion. If the spirits become angered or displeased, the people will not receive the blessings of the *gut* performed that day. From the very beginning of my career as a *mudang*, I received praise for skillfully riding the *jakdu* blades. During the height of my popularity, I would perform a *gut* at least every three days and ride *jakdu* as often.

One incident occurred when I was performing a *gut* in Osan. On that day, the Warrior God had descended powerfully within me. Holding the sacred warrior sword, I danced vigorously as if encountering and defeating enemies on the battlefield. The local people were mesmerized by this rare spectacle of a *gut*. Finally, it was time for me to climb onto the wooden platform with the *jakdu*. I touched the blades to my tongue, then to my cheek, and glided them along my arms and knees. But when I brought them to my shins, blood suddenly started flowing, staining my socks. There was no doubt that taboos had been violated. I quickly went to the kitchen, placed the *jakdu* knives in front of the hearth, and cleansed the impurities by dissolving the ashes in a bowl of water. Then I carefully lifted the *jakdu* onto my shoulders and returned to the courtyard.

"How appalling! There has been impurity!" I announced. "Who had the audacity to violate the taboos when the *jakdu* knives were sharpened? Confess immediately!" An enraged voice erupted from my mouth. The sounds of drums and gongs ceased, and the *gut* platform fell silent like a still pond.

"Confess and make amends swiftly, or else you shall witness the fury of my spirits, and it will be too late. Hurry and prostrate yourself in repentance!"

The elderly folks, who well knew the power and impact of the *gut*, were restless with anxiety and glanced nervously in all directions.

"Oh my, who is it? Come out quickly! The gods are furious! Why doesn't the guilty party come out at once and kneel, begging for forgiveness?"

At that moment, a young woman from the neighboring house stepped into the courtyard, trembling like a frightened cat that had fallen into water. The onlookers were confused, unsure of what had happened.

Just before the passage of *jakdu*, one of my *gut* team members was sharpening the knives in a separate room. The person sharpening the blades had folded the paper known as *hami* in his mouth, symbolizing the need to align the mind and body and refrain from speaking in thoughts and words. Unfortunately, it was precisely at that moment that the woman from the neighboring house opened the door to the room and witnessed the scene.

"Oh my, what on earth are you doing?"

Upon seeing the person with a blank piece of paper in his mouth, sharpening the *jakdu* blades, the woman burst into laughter. Taken aback by her, the person sharpening the knives vigorously shook his head at her. The woman quickly closed the door and left, but it was already too late.

"Oh dear, I have committed a grave sin. I truly didn't know what was going on. Please forgive me." With tears streaming down her face, the woman bowed countless times before the *chilseongdan*.

After she fervently prayed and turned away, I felt a sensation of lightness in my body. Placing the *jakdu* blades back in their position, I leaped onto them, and the people gathered breathed a collective sigh of relief.

Mudangs bestow *gongsu* oracles from atop the *jakdu* knives— messages from the spirits delivered to the people to reveal upcoming calamities and blessings and teach right from wrong.

The strict and commanding style of delivering *gongsu* is called *heulim gongsu*. During *heulim gongsu*, *mudangs* pour out rebukes and commands, and the people gathered around tremble and pray for forgiveness. The gods, who are benevolent and compassionate, quickly resolve their anger and promise to offer blessings and longevity. From time to time, the spirits offer oracles that point out wrongdoings and reprimand people.

"Do not be so greedy and think only of yourself."

"Do not hate others, but try to understand them and be considerate."

Similarly, oracles are also offered to provide strength during difficult times.

"You have experienced all kinds of suffering. After this last hurdle, you will be able to live well with peace of mind and good health."

"Your son is causing you deep pain. Nevertheless, embrace and nurture him well. There will come a day when his heart will change, and he will be a great son to you."

Could there be anyone not strengthened by receiving such words of hope from the spirits, even in times of great crisis?

It is vital to receive the oracles when they are given. When a *mudang* delivers *gongsu* oracles, one must step forward without hesitation and ask questions if there are uncertainties. Messages are not fabricated by the *mudangs* but are words bestowed by the gods to assist the people. If you ask about the message later, you have failed to receive the given oracle. When offering oracles, the *mudang* must be careful not to wield the words of the spirits recklessly. It is the role and responsibility of the *mudang*, as the intermediary between gods and humans, to deliver the oracles carefully so people can be guided.

THIRTY-FIVE

Receive Life and Share Blessings

My current home is situated on a steep hillside. Those who visit for the first time often struggle to drive their cars, as they cannot turn around on the hillside and sometimes have to navigate the steep road in reverse. Moreover, some people are taken aback by seeing my small and modest home.

"Who would believe a famous shaman like you lives here?"

Perhaps they expected a renowned *mudang* recognized by the government to reside in a grander home. However, outside the world of Spirit, I am quite foolish. Despite gaining fame and having performed significant *guts* for a long time, I have not been able to accumulate much wealth. For a long time, my aspiration has been to build a nursing home or an orphanage to provide care for lonely individuals with nowhere to go and live together with them there.

After returning from my 1982 performance in the United States, I had the opportunity to showcase *gut* performances in various countries. Unexpectedly, there was great foreign interest in traditional Shamanic practices. As someone who had experienced indifference and disparagement towards Shamanism in my own country, I was truly invigorated and encouraged to receive such welcome and acknowledgment abroad. It also reinforced my deep sense of responsibility to preserve and present our traditional Shamanic practices.

In line with this vision, I established Keumhwa-dang on Ganghwa Island. Keumhwa-dang serves as a training center dedicated to the preservation of intangible cultural assets. The space aims to preserve and promote the *Seohaean Poongeoje*, *Baeyonshin-gut*, and *Daedong-gut* rituals through extensive research and educational endeavors. Furthermore, I harbored ambitious plans to foster international exchange and training programs with other nations, with a particular emphasis on Indigenous Shamanic practices. As a result, the inauguration of the "*Seohaean Poongeoje*, *Baeyonshin-gut*, and *Daedong-gut* Preservation Association" coincided with the establishment of Keumhwa-dang.

Yet it was no easy task for a *mudang*, ignorant of the world's ways, to build such a place. I faced challenges and setbacks during the construction, and encountered difficulties with the workers. There were even times when construction had to be halted. Feeling defeated and uncertain of its completion, I would gaze down from the hill of Keumhwa-dang and ponder my woes. Thoughts such as: *Is this all I have achieved after decades of hardship and hunger?* would crowd my mind, leaving me frustrated and ashamed.

After many twists and turns, Keumhwa-dang was finally completed on March 23, 2004. I could finally take in the surroundings on the day of the *gosa* blessing ritual. From Keumhwa-dang, one could glimpse the distant sea where the sun sets. Perhaps because of this, I feel immersed in an indescribable sacred energy when I sit in the dark Samshin Hall at night. The Big Dipper shines faintly in the night sky while the bright moonlight reflects like a radiant lantern in each direction. As I gaze at this breathtaking view, I murmur, "Ah, I now understand why Great Spirit has chosen this place," and bow my head.

Keumhwa-dang was constructed through the sincere dedication of many people. Thanks to those who contributed, ranging from a few thousand to several tens of millions of *won*, the space became a reality. The essence of their generosity is engraved in every brick and beam. Even now, I find strength in the unwavering support of those who care, even if it is just for a single brick. However, if there is still a burden in my heart, it is the unfinished tasks that were initially planned during the construction of Keumhwa-dang. I aspire to build a *Chilseong* shrine next to the Samshin Hall and create a folk museum that beautifully displays Korea's cultural artifacts. Despite the challenges, I am determined to complete these endeavors and ensure our Indigenous folk traditions are properly preserved for future generations.

Every morning, I go to the shrine and offer earnest prayers.

"I pray for the good health and prosperity of all those who have supported Keumhwa-dang. May they be blessed abundantly. Please grant greater strength and courage to this humble disciple as I seek to complete Keumhwa-dang. May our country establish a peaceful and stable foundation so that all the people of Korea can be healthy and happy."

The doors of Keumhwa-dang are always wide open, so I hope anyone passing by will stop in to receive the blessings and grace that I, Kim Keum-Hwa, offer.

THIRTY-SIX

Ommai, My Beloved Ommai

"Ommai!"

Whenever I call for my mother, my heart constricts, my nostrils tingle, and my throat stiffens. I long to hear her respond, "Yes, I am here," even just once. I wish to hold onto my mother's slender wrist for a moment. How wonderful would that be?

My mother holds a profound place in my heart. My heart aches when I think about how much she must have suffered and how many tears she shed throughout her life, witnessing her own mother and later her daughter living as shamans.

When I was young, I thought my mother was a cruel person. She would make me carry my younger siblings on my back and forbid me from setting them down, and once, she mercilessly hit me on my head with a plastic bowl for stealing food from my grandmother. I had concluded that my mother didn't love her children at all. Yet, at the same time, I would often cry and long for her embrace. It was only as I grew older and became a woman myself that I was able to catch a glimpse of my mother's life. I began to understand how difficult and challenging her life must have been: worrying about how to put food on the table as soon as she woke up and taking on the responsibility of caring for an entire family after losing her husband at such a young age.

When I tasted something new and delicious for the first time on the plane to the United States, my mother was the first person that came to mind. Widowed at thirty-seven, she had never been on a plane herself, let alone enjoyed a bowl of cold noodles in peace, as she was busy raising her five children. The image of my mother, who couldn't even finish the *bulgogi* I occasionally treated her to, bringing it home tightly wrapped in newspaper, wrenched my heart. Watching her, I promised myself that I would treat her to delicious and exclusive food and, if not in the United States, at least on a trip to Jeju Island.

Until the day she passed away, my mother had pride and compassion for her daughter, a *mudang*. When I returned from my performances in the United States, my mother proudly proclaimed to the people in our neighborhood as I carried her on my back, "Look here, everyone. My daughter went all the way to America to perform *guts!*"

For my mother, it was a source of great pride that her *mudang* daughter took an airplane and went all the way to the United States to represent her country.

As mentioned, when I performed a *Mansudaetak-gut* at our home years ago, we were unable to complete the *gut* due to police harassment and chased away to the nearby Samgak Mountain. I couldn't let my exhausted mother walk on the dark mountain path, so she rode on my back that day as well. My mother felt as light as a feather, frail and thin. Only when we reached the top of the mountain did my mother get off my back.

After gazing down the mountain for a while, my mother spoke with great effort.

"You have traveled so far."

I was both my mother's greatest pride and hottest tear.

When my mother passed, I happened to be far away at Hawangdeung Island, assisting my spirit daughter, Hiah, in filming a movie. Before leaving for the island, I had tried my best to give my mother a nutrient injection because I had been worried about her health, but she adamantly refused to receive it.

"What's the point of getting that? I need to stop being a burden to you and go on my way."

One night during the shoot, I had a dream in which my mother waved her thin hand at me and said, "Do not follow." Even in the dream, I felt anxious, as if my mother would leave me. So, even after returning to the island, I would fetch fresh water every morning to pray for her. It was because I was not ready to let go of my mother yet.

One day, Hiah, observing me, said, "It's time to allow your mother to move on."

Was it my own selfishness that held onto my mother? Even if one lived in a field of dung, wouldn't it be better than the afterlife? Finally, one day, while praying, I burst into tears.

"*Ommai*, if you haven't been able to leave because of this unworthy daughter, I have sinned. You have suffered so much because of your mother and because of me, enduring a lifetime of pain and heartache. Please go to paradise and enjoy all the good things in the afterlife. I will let you go. Fly away in peace, like a crane, like a butterfly."

I can't even begin to describe how much I cried that day. Even though I knew I had to let my mother go, I still didn't want to say goodbye to her. Just a few days later, I received a call from my home in Seoul.

"Elder Kim Keum-Hwa…"

From the voice of the person who called, I could sense that my mother had passed away. I quickly packed my belongings and hailed a taxi. Only in the cab did I realize I was wearing mismatched shoes—a man's rubber shoe on the right and a woman's rubber shoe on the left.

There was a time when my mother unexpectedly asked me to buy her Western-style shoes. My mother had always dressed in traditional Korean clothes and traditionally wore her hair, but she suddenly desired to try on a blouse and a skirt. At that time, I refused to buy her the shoes, fearing the criticism of others. Now, I would have purchased them ten times over, regardless of what others might say. However, there is no use in regretting a hundred times when she is no longer here.

After my mother passed, my heart was plagued with endless regrets. Every time I went to the market and saw shrimp or the *injeolmi* rice cakes she loved, tears would well up in my eyes. I regretted not preparing her favorite dishes more often while she was alive, and a sense of loss and grief overwhelmed me. I couldn't even fulfill my promise of taking her on a plane trip—my mother, who was so happy just being carried on my back.

Whenever I heard songs about mothers, tears would flow uncontrollably. When I returned home after being out, I would find myself heading toward my mother's room.

"*Ommai!*"

As I reached for the doorknob, calling out for her, I suddenly remembered, "Oh, my mother is not here anymore," and my hopelessness was indescribable. I longed so much for my mother's warm hands pulling me to the heated floor after I'd attended a prayer ritual and returned home late in the cold winter, saying, "Put your feet between mine. You're a block of ice."

At home, I was haunted by thoughts of my mother, so one day, I just showed up at my friend's house. My friend was surprised to see me so dejected and devoid of energy.

"What's wrong?"

"I can't stay home because I keep thinking about my mother."

Even though I knew it was pointless, I couldn't let go of the desire to hear my mother's voice once again, to catch a glimpse of her, even if it was just her profile. Even though I was surrounded by a powerful spiritual presence, my mother's absence felt immense.

Even now, on days when my heart feels heavy and life seems hard, I deeply miss my mother. In those moments, I quietly call out to her.

"*Ommai.*"

When my mother was alive, whenever I would vent to her about difficult or painful things, she would gently pat my back and comfort me.

"Child, why allow those ugly people and their behavior to get to you? Just leave them be."

With that one sentence, the unbearable anguish I felt dissolved. "You're right. Why should I waste my heart on such petty matters?"

With that, I would brush it off. How did my mother, who was not a *mudang*, know how to offer such profound comfort? Perhaps it was her subtle way of teaching me to become a person who can provide solace to others. Maybe my mother is still watching over me with a warm smile. I miss her to the very core of my bones.

West Sea Abundant Fishing and Village Ritual

Kim Keum-Hwa performing a ritual at Dr. Zo Zayong's Emile Museum in 1981. She is doing a blessing in front of a *chilseongdan*, before she mounts the *jakdu* blades.

Kim Keum-Hwa with her mother and two scholars of Korean Shamanism dressed in the Shamanic attire, circa 1980s. Mother was very proud to witness her daughter be sought out by the scholars both in and outside of Korea.

Previous page: Kim Keum-Hwa during a *Daedong-gut* mounting *jakdu* blades in 2001. Her niece Kim Hye-Kyoung is nearby providing assistance.

Kim Keum-Hwa in a group photo with other religious workers and spiritual leaders, circa 1980s. Her work has contributed to elevating Korean Shamanism into a faith tradition that deserves respect as other religions.

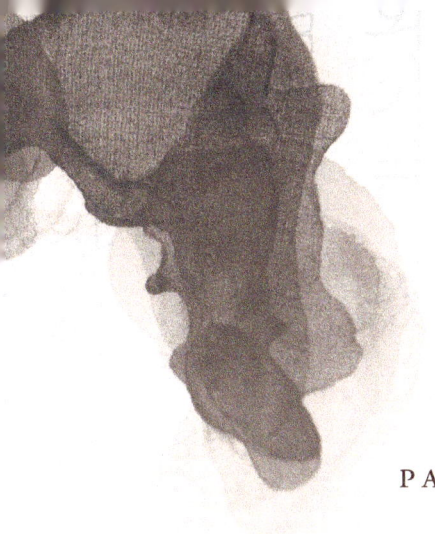

PART 5

Following the Mudang's Path

All in all, Divine Spirit is timeless and eternal. There will always be *mudangs* who are called to walk the paths guided by Spirit.

by Kim Hye-Kyoung

THIRTY-SEVEN

My *Gomo*, My Aunt Kim Keum-Hwa

As a child, I remember my *gomo* as intimidating.

My father died suddenly when I was seven years old, and my siblings and I were sent to my aunt to live with her and her mother for a few years. My mother had to work very hard for a few years to establish a stable home so our family could be reunited. My mother eventually got a home in the same neighborhood and brought us to live with her. Because of these years living with and around my aunt, I witnessed my aunt's life as a *mudang* all my life.

My aunt must have been able to see something in me—a spirit calling, spirit energy. While I had no specific symptoms, she would often say to me, "You will follow my path." I hated hearing that. When I returned from school each day, I often found her standing on top of the *jakdu* blade, in ritual. Upon seeing me, channeling one of her gods, she loudly proclaimed that I would follow her path. This was in the years when shamans were discriminated against and persecuted in Korea, when police officers would barge into *gut* rituals to arrest *mudangs*, so witnessing my aunt's hardships—watching her embodiment by gods during rituals and being chased by police—scared me. I hated my up-close view of the difficulties of a *mudang's* life.

"If I have to become a *mudang*, I will just drink poison and kill myself," I used to say. "I will never be a *mudang*."

But Divine Spirit had a plan for me that I could not resist. At twenty-eight years old and a young mother of two children, spirits descended on me. All of a sudden, my body began shaking, I had a constant headache, and my chest felt like it might explode. When I was in one of these fits, I—who did not normally drink alcohol—could drink a whole bottle of whiskey alone. Yet I wouldn't act drunk, only strange. I often spoke about nonsensical things, even sharing what I knew of my neighbors' intimate secrets and situations.

When I lay down, I would see my Aunt Kim Keum-Hwa dressed in her white *sobok*, sitting next to my bedside. Sometimes, I found myself outside, holding onto a large earthen clay pot and laughing loudly about how pleased I was with it. In the middle of the night, I would call my mother, insisting I could not stand because I was being pressed down by something. Yet I also insisted that I must talk to a particular neighbor because another was sick, that one person needed to watch out for an accident, while another would soon come upon money. In this crazed and erratic state, I began giving *gongsu* to the neighbors. Before long, people who heard of me started showing up at our house asking for a reading.

My mother must have had some intuition that I would eventually become a *mudang*. Not only had she heard my aunt giving *gongsu* for many years that I would follow her own path, but my mother also had a series of ominous dreams over the years. In one, she dreamed that I walked through their front door carrying on my head a large bundle of Shamanic tools and attire needed for a *gut* performance. Behind me, a line of old women walked in, seemingly my customers. After these dreams, she would call me, asking if I felt all right or ill, even years before my spirit sickness started. So when I began suffering the *shinbyeong*—showing the signs of becoming a *mudang*—my mother led me to Seoul, where my aunt Kim Keum-Hwa was living at the time.

"It took you long enough," she said when she saw I'd finally arrived at her house. That's how I received the *Naerim-gut* from my aunt and became one of her many spirit daughters.

Even before I was officially initiated to walk the path of a *mudang*, my gods were already guiding me. A few weeks before my initiation ritual, I visited a property on Mount Manwolsan to attend another shaman's ritual. While I was there, I became embodied by a Grandfather Spirit—walking up to the elderly lady who owned the property, like an old man, speaking in an old man's voice and tone. I demanded the old lady give me one of the hens at the property. She refused, saying it was too valuable a breed to give away, and I, getting frustrated and impatient, yelled in an old man's voice that I had business to do with the chicken, but since she was refusing it, I was not pleased. After my outburst, I left.

When such embodiment and channeling happen, a *mudang*'s own consciousness takes a backseat. While a *mudang* is aware that an embodiment and channeling of spirit is occurring, when it does, we lose control of our own bodies and simply become observers. When the Grandfather Spirit demanded the offering of chicken, my young, inexperienced self had no idea what I would have done with it if it had been given to me. I only know the Grandfather Spirit would have known what to do, and I would have followed his guidance. Only after the gods finally leave my body can I return to myself, remembering and marveling at the actions and words I so freely shared.

Months later, after I received my own *Naerim-gut* and started my work as a shaman, a man came looking for me. He was the son of the old grandmother at the mountain house, from whom I had requested the chicken. He had asked if I was the *mudang* who demanded a donation of one of the property's hens, explaining his mother had fallen ill shortly after our encounter and was not getting better. He wanted to know what he had to do to heal his mother. I responded that the timing had been lost, and I didn't see any way to undo the illness. Had I received the chicken in the first place, the Grandfather Spirit embodying me would have known what to do and guided me. Looking back, I imagine I might have performed a type of *daesudaemyeong* sacrificial ritual to transfer the grandmother's illness and ill fortune to the chicken instead, protecting her from harm. But once divine timing is lost and the opportunity to be dutiful to Divine Spirit is refused, even powerful *mudangs* cannot undo what was left to occur later.

It is an exercise of letting go and surrendering; we can't force people to follow the spirits' guidance, just as we can't force spirits to achieve a specific outcome or negotiate with them to ensure the outcome we wish for our clients. To do this work requires a devout faith in the Divine and a profound letting go—acceptance that even as a *mudang*, one can only achieve so much. Ultimately, what happens is up to Spirit. Divine guidance is sometimes absolute, and it's hard to intervene after Spirit's timing has passed. As sad and frustrating as it can be to discover a client has suffered the consequences of not following Divine guidance, understanding that reality and surrendering to it—following the flow of what will be—is also an essential part of the job of a *mudang*. It is our fate.

THIRTY-EIGHT

My Spirit Mother, My Teacher Kim Keum-Hwa

Walking the path of *mudang* under the guidance of my aunt—my spirit mother—was grueling and difficult. As a child, growing up under her roof, my aunt seemed scary, cold, and distant, always so sensitive to sound that it was difficult for her to tolerate the noises other people made. We were all very poor before my aunt began receiving national and global recognition for her Shamanic performances. There was not enough to eat, and she scolded us for eating too much or trying to take portions of her mother's favorite food at the meal table—she was frugal and stern. That didn't change when I became her spirit daughter.

As my spirit mother and teacher, she was demanding in her instruction of the Shamanic songs and dances that comprised the various *guts* we performed. In addition to learning the *guts*, there was so much work involved in cooking and preparing the offering foods for each performance. Absolute obedience was expected, and she was especially hard on me. I cried a lot, thinking she didn't really like me and was not pleased with me. But looking back now, I can see she was especially hard on me in order to strengthen and fortify me for the challenges and hardships that lay in my future as the successor of her path and legacy. Now I know she tried to prepare me for this lonely, difficult path of succeeding her.

After my father passed, Aunt Kim Keum-Hwa used to say that my siblings and I should think of her as our father. But she seemed so difficult to approach, so hard to get close to. It was only after I began to grow older myself, fifteen years before her own death, that she and I started opening our hearts to one another, becoming warmer and enjoying each other as family. It might have helped that she eventually began to see me as a good *mudang*—she started sending me some of her regular customers for Shamanic work, and we performed together many times after that.

Aunt Kim Keum-Hwa used to say that our work—Korean Shamanism, *gut* rituals, connecting with Divine Spirit, using our tools to heal others—was our roots and soul. We firmly believed we needed to preserve our traditions and protect them all the time in all that we did. She also instilled in us, her spirit daughters, the value of humility. No matter how much fame came her way or how her financial situation improved over time, my aunt herself never changed. Even with her success and recognition, she was never wealthy, always pinching pennies and often sitting alone in her dark house to conserve energy. She told us that she was not rich even after seventy years of Shamanic work, even after receiving the designation of one of Korea's Important Intangible Cultural Assets.

She emphasized the importance of respecting elders and treating others with respect and politeness, teaching us to offer our work to those in need who may not be able to pay for our rituals or services. Especially on *Ipchun* (a Korean holiday that falls right after the first full moon of the Lunar Year and marks the beginning of spring) and *Chilseok* (Lunar July 7th, when yin and yang are in balance), we offered rituals, *Bujeok* sigil, and prayer blessings to the community without accepting much payment. When encountering people suffering from spirit-related issues and unable to afford the cost of the proper *gut*, my aunt often did the work while only charging the cost of supplies and food.

My aunt didn't believe in *mudangs* recommending the performance of *gut* ceremonies too often or too frequently, merely to make money. She told us to use discernment, perform the ritual, and wait awhile to see if it was effective. She was against repeatedly selling the same goods and services to the same client for the same outcome, saying the frequency of a ritual's performance didn't guarantee that it would be effective. Instead, she emphasized recommending and performing *gut* rituals with a purity of intention and a full-hearted connection to Divine Spirit. It was our tradition to honor the community with our work.

For much of her life, Kim Keum-Hwa was a famous public figure, often surrounded by people and in the spotlight, but I remember her as someone who felt loneliness deeply. She was sensitive, childlike, and could be quite solitary. She used to love being surrounded by her spirit daughters whenever we gathered to prepare for a performance, joyful and happy like a child, immersed in people who understood her work and her path. But once everyone returned home, she was alone. No matter how many people might be gathered for a ritual or in the audience of a performance, how many admirers and visitors, students, and family might be around, ultimately, a *mudang's* life is a lonely one. The *mudang* is always walking their path alone, accompanied only by spirits. The only people who understand this isolated path of the *mudang* are those few also walking the same path.

It is a path Kim Keum-Hwa walked her entire life; one she knew more intimately than any other.

I also understand the loneliness of this path, even though I have a family who support my work as a Korean shaman. As a *mudang*, I must follow the Divine Spirit's guidance, which is usually the most important priority. Spirit's guidance is never planned or arranged according to mundane human expectations, and this obedience and surrendering to Spirit can cause conflicts with family and friends. It is difficult to anticipate Spirit's guidance and plan ahead. It must be frustrating to have their mother, wife, or sister who misses out on family events or must reprioritize obligations because Spirit has let her know she must go to the mountains or begin a prayer ritual that will last many nights.

Mudangs can't sleep when everyone else does because we often pray to gods late at night or early in the morning. On big holidays like *Chuseok* and *Seollal*, when everyone is enjoying their time with family, we often work on rituals, make offerings to the gods, and perform blessings for clients. We never get to live the ordinary lives of others.

These feelings of otherness and loneliness can only be understood by other shamans who experience similar challenges. We also appreciate the incredible awe and gratitude of working with powerful gods and spirits and the rewarding feelings of serving others by doing this work. Our profound interactions with the gods and clients—as well as the fears, worries, sufferings, and joys of walking the path of our work—can't be understood by laypeople. Only other *mudangs* or those on a similar journey can understand our experience—that's why the spirit family and the support and community of other spirit workers are essential for shamans.

THIRTY-NINE

Protecting Her Legacy into the Future

I became my aunt's legal successor in 2014, in charge of continuing the legacy of her Intangible Cultural Property of the West Sea *Baeyonshin-gut* and her shrine, Keumhwa-dang. There are still many challenges in doing this work; there are people who still challenge the Shamanic cultural property and the estate of Keumhwa-dang.

My aunt had groomed many *mudangs* in her long career, and many have become very successful on their own merits. There are some who feel they are more deserving of the title of a successor and are displeased that it was given to a family member. But through the hard work and training my aunt put me through, I am holding down the fort firmly to honor Kim Keum-Hwa's last words and wish to have her family keep her legacy.

In the last few years of her life, knowing she suffered from illness and many other health issues, my aunt offered clear direction on how she would like her legacy to be preserved.

One particular cemetery is popular among those who left

North Korea because it overlooks the faraway homeland. My aunt told us that she did not want to be buried in that cemetery—or any cemetery at all. She said, "Who would visit me after death? At a cemetery, no less? If anyone visits, it would most likely be another shaman, so I want to be at Keumhwa-dang." When she was sick and knew she would pass soon, she asked us to cremate her body and sprinkle her ashes on the mountain behind Keumhwa-dang, leaving her a memorial stone somewhere on the property. That's exactly what we did.

She asked to never let go of Keumhwa-dang—never to sell or give it to someone else. She wanted her name, Kim Keum-Hwa, to be preserved forever. She asked that Keumhwa-dang stay in the family and be protected into the future—were someone outside of the family to be named the successor, it could eventually threaten her legacy, should they wish to change the name of the shrine, become unwilling to do the work and spend the money needed to upkeep and maintain such property, or be invested in establishing their own fame and reputation instead of preserving hers. For all these reasons, my aunt entrusted this responsibility to her family.

One of my main goals in maintaining my aunt's legacy is renovating and expanding Keumhwa-dang. When she was alive, my aunt dreamed of preserving her Shamanic tools, paintings, and other *gut*-related artifacts in a cultural museum and opening the property to visitors from Korea and abroad. She wanted to create a place where foreigners could visit and learn about "our roots and soul," as she called Korean Shamanism. She did not live to see this accomplishment to its completion, so now, I have taken on the vision.

I want to expand Keumhwa-dang and build more individual shrines for additional Shamanic deities and gods, such as *Dangun* and *Divine King Chiwoo*. Similar to the Buddhist temples in Korea serving as sanctuaries and Buddhist educational centers for visitors, I would like to make Keumhwa-dang a place for healing and learning about Korea's ancestral wisdom, where people can come watch *gut* performances, learn about their ancestral culture, and even pray and show respect to these powerful gods and spirits.

I don't know if I or my family will have the resources and capabilities to make my aunt's dream come true, but I am committed to dedicating my life to manifesting this mission.

Compared to the past, when my aunt experienced so much discrimination and persecution, times have changed, and there are many *mudangs* in Korea right now—our work is being recognized for its cultural importance and ability to help people. Like other professionals, some *mudangs* are good, some are bad, and many fall somewhere in between.

Unlike other religions currently recognized in Korea, Korean Shamanism lacks structure and organization. Because each *mudang's* path is individualized, guided only by their spirits, it is difficult to find commonality and cohesion among Korean shamans. But this, too, is slowly changing. Some universities offer training curriculums about Korean Shamanism for the benefit of *mudangs* as well as the education of the public.

My hope is that this type of effort will pay off, and eventually, Korean Shamanism will be accepted and recognized as a religion or spiritual tradition in Korea.

All in all, Divine Spirit is timeless and eternal. There will always be *mudangs* who are called to walk the paths guided by Spirit. I hope in fifty or one hundred years, their paths will be less rough, less filled with prejudice and struggles, and that *mudangs* will be respected and supported as spiritual practitioners doing meaningful and vital spiritual work, not unlike Christian pastors and Buddhist monks.

I have initiated many people onto their Shamanic path with *Naerim-gut*. Almost all who come to me for initiation have long suffered from *shinbyeong*, or spirit sickness, affecting their physical and mental health. Sometimes, their suffering is from Spirit's influence on their financial, familial, or occupational situations, and they are distraught. Everyone's journey is different, but they often find healing and clarity after their *Naerim-gut*.

Many of these prospective *mudangs* do end up following a path of a *mudang*, often working under me for many years—as much as ten or even twenty. Others leave to do their work independently. But not everyone who gets *Naerim-gut* walks the traditional path of a *mudang* like my aunt, me, and many of our spirit daughters. Once they find relief from their spirit sickness and get clarity on their path, they return to their former professions. They continue to serve their gods and maintain their shrines, but their approach doesn't always include performing *gongsu* and *gut*.

Some of the women I have worked with are of the Korean diaspora and suffering from the trauma of adoption and/or immigration, and they receive healing from the Shamanic rituals. For these spirit daughters, I am unable to teach and mentor them as I would others, due to the language barrier. But I try to instill courage and continued faith in trusting their gods and following their guidance.

When I look back on my aunt's life, I see her always praying for others. I now realize that living entirely on behalf of others is truly an amazing legacy. She was a healer of sicknesses of body and heart, dedicating her life to reducing other people's suffering. She was also a sage advisor, guiding people in their life decisions. She was a dancer and *gut* performer who used music and dance to release suffering and negative energies, celebrate life, and inspire joy. Divine Spirit is truly light energy, and my aunt channeled this light in everything she did. When people received her light, they felt warm and healed, no matter their culture, background, or race.

The story of my aunt, Kim Keum-Hwa, is that of a *mudang's* path and a *mudang's* work. I hope everyone who reads this book will appreciate learning about her life, her challenges, and her immense gifts. My wish is that the readers of this book will feel the *jeong* and light Kim Keum-Hwa offered to others all her life. I hope readers of this book receive the healing and blessings of Divine Spirit that my aunt worked to cultivate.

There is no tree without roots. Everyone has ancestors from whom their own lives originated, even if they may feel disconnected from their families and heritage. In the spirit of continuing to branch out from my own ancestry, I promise to proceed on the path Kim Keum-Hwa tread before me, protecting this work as she did and as she taught me to. Please be open and accepting of this gift. I hope this book serves as a healing balm, an encouragement, and a blessing.

This book is a gift to the people ...

"Here comes life, here come blessings.
Everlasting medicine from the Samshin mountain is coming,
Good fortune is coming; health, too.
Here come blessings to those who read this book.
May you be at peace, and may your wishes come true.
This manshin Kim Hye-Kyoung prays and blesses you with
a long, healthy life and happiness."

명이 가요, 복이 가요.
삼신산에는 불로초가 가고 재수가 갑니다.
건강이 가요, 축원이 갑니다.
이 책을 보시는 분 평안하고 소원성취 무병장수 기원합니다.
김혜경 축원을 드립니다.

Top photo: Kim Hye-Kyoung leading a *gut* passage of spirit blessings on stage while Kim Keum-Hwa observes and assists.

Bottom photo: Kim Hye-Kyoung in a *gut* performance. She continues to follow the traditional styles and passages of the Shamanic rituals she learned from her spirit mother and aunt, Kim Keum-Hwa.

Kim Keum-Hwa made her niece and spirit daughter Kim Hye-Kyoung as her official successor. Here pictured during one of many *gut* performances together.

Kim Keum-Hwa and Kim Hye-Kyoung as an aunt and a niece in plain clothes, circa 2009.

About the Authors

Nara Manshin Kim Keum-Hwa (나라만신 김금화) was born in Hwanghae province of North Korea in 1931. At seventeen years old she received an initiation ritual to become a *mudang*, a Korean shaman. During the Korean war she moved to South Korea and since then dedicated herself in her work as a shaman as well as preserving and sharing the art of Korean Shamanic rituals (*guts*) to the world. She received the designation of one of Korea's Important Intangible Cultural Assets in 1985 and continued her work as the nation's most recognized shaman until her death in 2019.

Hyekyoung-gung Manshin Kim Hye-Kyoung (혜경궁 김혜경 만신) was born in Inchon, South Korea in 1962. At the age of 29, she received an initiation ritual by her aunt Kim Keum-Hwa and became a *mudang*. She assisted and worked with Kim Keum-Hwa in efforts of preserving and performing *Seohaean Baeyeonshin-gut* and *Daedong-gut* (the Abundant Fishing and Village Ritual of the West Sea). She became the official successor of Kim Keum-Hwa in 2014 and has served as the president of the Preservation Society of *Seohaean Baeyeonshin-gut* and *Daedong-gut* since 2015. She received the official recognition as the educator of Korea's Important Intangible Cultural Asset in 2020, and continues her work within and outside of Korea. Visit mudang.org for more information.

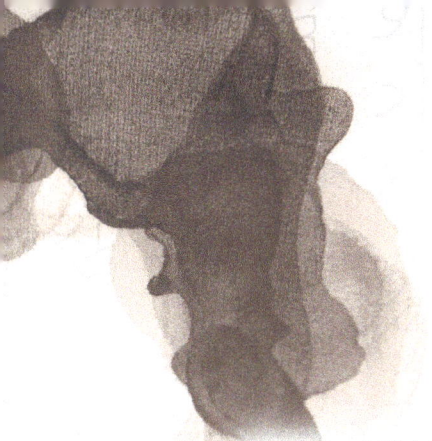